AMBI PARAMESWARAN

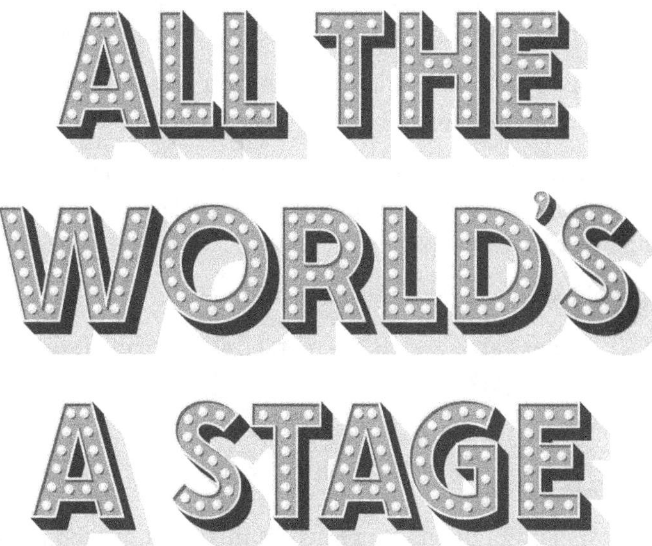

A PERSONAL BRANDING STORY

First published by Westland Business, an imprint of Westland Books, a division of Nasadiya Technologies Private Limited, in 2022

No. 269/2B, First Floor, 'Irai Arul', Vimalraj Street, Nethaji Nagar, Allappakkam Main Road, Maduravoyal, Chennai 600095

Westland, the Westland logo, Westland Business and the Westland Business logo are the trademarks of Nasadiya Technologies Private Limited, or its affiliates.

ISBN: 9789395073684

10 9 8 7 6 5 4 3 2 1

Typeset by SÜRYA, New Delhi
Printed at Manipal Technologies Limited, Manipal

ALL THE WORLD'S A STAGE

Ambi Parameswaran is a brand coach and founder, brand-building.com, a brand advisory. He is a featured speaker at corporate events, a guest faculty at leading business schools and an award-winning bestselling author of eleven books. His specially curated workshop on Personal Branding has been very popular with both leading corporates and industry bodies.

Ambi has spent his forty-year career in corporate India working across diverse sectors, such as pharmaceuticals/consumer products (Boots Company), media (UDI Yellow Pages) and advertising (Rediffusion). He spent over twenty-five years with FCB Ulka Advertising, helping transform a struggling ad agency into one of the top five marketing communications groups. Over the last six years, turning independent, he has served as a member director on corporate and advisory boards, as a brand coach to small and large brands and as a mentor to exciting new businesses. He has, through his career and beyond, worked on iconic brands like Tata, Wipro, Zee, TCS, Amul, Tropicana, Pepsico, LIC, Santoor, Sundrop, Abbott, J&J, ITC, and so on.

Ambi now reads, writes, teaches and coaches leaders across multiple domains. He is a guest faculty at IIM Calcutta, IIM Ahmedabad, MICA and an Adjunct Professor of Marketing at SPJIMR Mumbai.

Ambi's columns appear regularly in *Business Standard* and in several other business publications including *Economic Times* and *The Hindu BusinessLine*. He is a distinguished alumnus award recipient from both IIT Madras and IIM Calcutta, an AMP Graduate from Harvard Business School, a PhD in Management from Mumbai University and a CFI certified CEO coach.

Ambi can be reached at ambimgp@brand-building.com. He is active on LinkedIn as Ambi Parameswaran and on Twitter as @ambimgp.

*Published as India celebrates its
75th year of independence,
this book is humbly dedicated to the
memory of Mahatma Gandhi,
the most enduring personal brand
to emerge out of India*

CONTENTS

A Disclaimer

THIS BOOK IS PRESENTED AS A CONVERSATION AMONG A group of friends from business school, who meet for their silver reunion back at their alma mater. All the characters here are figments of my imagination. In order to bring some semblance of reality, one of the characters is called Ambi. He is a lot younger than me, and purely imaginary too.

Two friends who meet at the reunion go on a walk and start conversing about branding and personal branding. They are joined by two more friends, and later by another one. As they dig deeper and deeper into the topic, there are several agreements, disagreements, arguments and insights. Over the course of this conversation, I have tried to present the many facets of how one can go about building one's personal brand.

This book is written to make it accessible for both the young and the not-so-young reader. Understanding of marketing or branding is not a prerequisite. While the setting is that of a business school, there is a conscious avoidance of any jargon.

The book ends with a short essay on possibly the most successful personal brand built in modern times—Mahatma Gandhi. Yes, while Mahatma Gandhi did not consciously go about building his personal brand, he ended up building one that continues to inspire and engage us all.

This book is dedicated to his memory.

Prologue

WHY IS AMBI WRITING ABOUT PERSONAL BRANDING?

How does this fit in with what he has been doing for the last forty plus years?

It is likely that you may have such questions going through your mind as you start reading this book. And you are right in asking these questions. I spent a large part of my career building brands. Somewhere in the process I realised that I also needed to build my ad agency's brand. Moreover, I figured out that to be amply successful in my day job, I needed to work on building my personal brand too. In the world of business, be it finance or marketing, customers want to deal with people who they respect. What is true in the world of business is also true in other domains, like education or public service or even in the NGO sector.

You might be wondering, like my friend in the book, isn't personal branding all about bragging and boasting? Well, not entirely. If done right, it is not about boasting or even humble bragging.

My effort at building my personal brand was a way of infusing some respect into my persona.

In a demanding full-time job, you hardly have the time to do your job wholly. Where, then, is the time to build your personal brand? But there are sustainable ways of doing it. For instance, over two decades ago, I realised that I like to teach and train. In my endeavour to be a better teacher, I started reading voraciously. I also realised that there was an acute paucity of Indian case studies to be used in teaching. So, I wrote two books of advertising case studies. In my desire to build my personal brand and that of the ad agency I worked in, I ensured that the books I wrote got covered by all the leading media vehicles of the time. Popular business magazines, newspapers and TV channels all covered these books, and thus my personal brand started getting some traction.

As my reputation grew, I got invited to write guest columns for newspapers. Remember this was all pro bono. I did not refuse any such invitation. I wrote for *The Economic Times, Business Line, Financial Express, Impact, The Week,* to name a few. I suppose what I wrote must have resonated well with the audience, and I started writing a regular column for *Mint* and then for *Business Standard.*

As my personal brand gathered some sheen, I started getting invitations to speak at industry forums. I made the time to keep these commitments, in addition to my work. Be it at the Confederation of Indian Industries (CII), Federation of Indian Chambers of Commerce & Industry (FICCI), Organisation of Pharmaceutical Producers of

India (OPPI), All India Management Association (AIMA), Madras Management Association (MMA), or the various others of which I have lost count, I took every one of my talks seriously. I curated the presentations thoroughly and tried to leave a good impression. For my agency's sake and for my own sake too.

I realised that joining some industry bodies will help my ad agency and me. I joined the Ad Club and later served as its president. Then came the Advertising Agencies Association of India, where too I was the president for two terms. I was invited to serve on the Board of Governors of IIM Calcutta. I also served on a few expert committees of the Bombay Chamber of Commerce, Indian Merchant Chambers (IMC), Securities and Exchange Board of India (SEBI) and CII.

When social media platforms like Facebook, LinkedIn and Twitter became popular, I joined these and made sure that I actively shared what I thought would be useful for my friends, associates, students and clients.

In the last twenty years, I have authored ten books and this is my eleventh book. I have also written two mini-books and over a hundred articles. All these undertakings to share my research and thoughts, and connecting with people, have helped me build my brand.

When I left my full-time job at FCB Ulka in 2016, I lost the clout and muscle that comes with the CEO tag. But my personal brand has stayed with me. And in several ways my personal brand has helped me stay relevant, get independent directorship on corporate boards, brand coaching engagements, teaching gigs, writing assignments, speaking opportunities and more.

Have I done a perfect job of building my personal brand? I don't think so. I could have done so much more and gotten more mileage. But that is one of life's truisms. In my case, in trying to balance working for a company, building its reputation, managing a happy family life and building my own personal brand, I think I managed to find a fine balance.

I hope this book will help you discover your fine balance too.

1

Are You Still Selling Dreams?

'ARRÉ, AMBI, STILL SELLING DREAMS?' I TURNED AROUND and saw Shankar Shah, leaning against the pillar outside the Management Development Centre, about to light a cigarette.

We were back on campus for our silver reunion, and this was probably the tenth time that Shankar had asked me the question in the last two days. As to why he had been ribbing me, the story goes back a few decades.

Shankar and I were classmates at IIM Calcutta, class of 1994. He was one of the top students in our class of around two hundred students. We both had engineering degrees. While Shankar chose to join a big automobile company to maximise his engineering and MBA education, I jumped ship and went to advertising—a field where I probably did not need an MBA, let alone my engineering degree.

While I went from advertising to marketing and back to advertising in the last twenty-five years, Shankar did something probably more respect-worthy. After starting his career with the auto major, he moved on in a few years to set up his own auto ancillary unit. In fact, his other founding partners were two of his erstwhile colleagues. They say a good start-up is successful not because of the core idea, but because the founding partners make a perfect team.

Starting small, supplying to the same company where they used to work, Shankar and his partners expanded slowly and soon became the go-to company for automotive gaskets of all kinds. After serving Indian companies well, they tapped into the global market. By 2017, they had reached a turnover of over Rs 700 crores. The company had a successful IPO (Initial Public Offering) in 2018 and Shankar was a very wealthy man. However, looking at him you would not be able to make this out. He still wore the same simple clothes that he used to, safari suits at times, carried an old mobile phone and lived in the same flat in Gurgaon that he had bought many years ago.

Shankar was of the opinion that advertising was all about stories and 'selling dreams' and hence he had been pulling my leg about this ever since I got into advertising. All these decades hadn't changed this about him.

We had finished dinner and it was our last night on campus. So, I suggested we go for a long walk around the campus and its seven lakes. He readily agreed, as long as I told him about the art of selling dreams. From the looks of it, he was not sleepy at all.

It was a cool December evening and the campus was relatively quiet since most of the students were off for their December break. There was a thin mist hanging in the air that made the atmosphere just right to talk about dreams.

'Hey Shankar, what do you know about the advertising business?' I asked. Having worked in advertising for over two decades I know that everyone and everyone's aunt has an opinion about every single ad they see on TV. I have had clients tell me, 'I like the ad, but would like to get a real consumer reaction to it.' The real consumer whom they were seeking an opinion from is often their spouse and kids!

I thought Shankar would be no different. Shankar's answer threw me. He said, 'I know very little about advertising since I don't need advertising in my line of work. I meet prospective customers, sell them my product with a strong sales pitch, technical specifications, client testimonials and I am usually very successful. In fact, I use all my engineering and business education to make the sale.' I nodded.

Then he threw me a zinger, 'Arré, you are an engineer and an MBA to boot. And you make ads. Yes, some of my customers use advertising to sell their products. But I am convinced that automobiles sell on their technical specifications, performance and based on the ads you create. I don't know enough about your business, but want to know more. What I see are ads on TV and the internet. But what larger purpose do they serve? And how are you using all that good education that you have under that greying mane of yours?'

I thought for a bit and realised that I needed to broaden

the topic of discussion. I asked him, 'Shankar, what is the brand by which your company is known to your customers?'

'That's easy,' he said. 'We're known by our company name, Perfect Gaskets. So that is also our brand, I should imagine. But how important is a brand? Where did the concept of branding come from?'

I decided to pose the question back to Shankar, 'What do you know about brands and branding?' To which his reply was candid, 'Very little, I think. I ducked most of the marketing courses, as you know. I am often confused between a brand and the name of a company. How are they different or similar?'

We had moved away from the Centre and were approaching the first lake. This lake was partly covered with weeds but we could see some bubbles in the water.

'Shankar, where do you think the word "brand" comes from?'

'Oh, that is easy. Branding, as a word, comes from the fact that in cattle ranches farmers used to brand their cattle with hot irons. Didn't we learn that in some class?'

'We did, but tell me the origin of the word "brand". As you know most words have a back story and the science of....'

'You mean entomology,' Shankar chipped in.

'Aah, got you there. Entomology is the study of insects. We are talking about etymology. So, what is the etymology of the word "brand"?'

'I have no idea. You are the expert. So, tell me.'

'Well, brand comes from the Old Norse word "brandr",

which means to burn. So, when we are building a brand, we are trying to burn a name in the minds of our customers.'

'Interesting, but painful. Ha ha! Did not know that brand comes from a burning origin. But is the idea of giving names and brands a recent practice or is it an old custom?'

'Archaeologists have found that even in prehistoric times, potters used to mark their name or symbol onto what they made. So, the idea of branding your produce is indeed an old custom. Patented medicine and packaged goods makers understood the power of brands early. According to popular folklore, branding, as we know it, started taking root in 1931, when a young Harvard MBA, McElroy, wrote to his managers in Procter & Gamble that the time was right to create "brand men" and a brand manager system.'

'What? And until then who was managing all those great brands of P&G like Camay and Ivory?' Shankar asked.

'Well, those days they had what was known as a promotions department. It was McElroy who conceptualised the idea of a brand manager. His three-page memo is a classic on what a brand management function is expected to do. I believe he even got featured in *Time* magazine!' I replied. 'And in marketing studies, there has been a lot of research around brands and branding in the last fifty years or so.'

Shankar nodded wisely and asked his next question 'Now I get why branding is such a big deal in packaged consumer product companies. They are all emulating what P&G started. I suppose the brand management concept then jumped from the FMCG sector to other sectors. But will this stay the same? Does branding matter in this new age? Customers know so much from the internet. Won't they figure out that the actual difference between brands is very little, and may be nothing more than the dreams that you ad guys are selling?'

I laughed and asked Shankar, 'Hey, are you sure your name is not Naomi Klein?'

'Hain, who is that?' Shankar asked.

'Well, Naomi Klein wrote a book in 1999 called *No Logo*. In that book she predicted that brands were on their last leg. Consumers will not fall for the dreams being sold to them. They will decide what they want without the trappings of a brand halo. Look at it this way. Most consumers know that the Nike they buy for say Rs 10,000 is made in China and was probably sourced for Rs 2,000 or less. She hypothesised that once a consumer knew this, why would they not switch to a cheaper store brand. But that did not happen. Interestingly, *The Economist* did a cover story in 2001 called "Pro Logo".'

'And what did *The Economist* have to say?' asked Shankar.

'The article said that brands are as loved by their consumers, as by the creators or manufacturers. They are not going to go away any time soon. Consumers are not ignorant when they pay Rs 10,000 for a pair of shoes that may only be marginally better than a store brand that is retailing at Rs 2,000. But they want to pay that extra to be doubly sure that they are getting the right quality. And add to that the flash value of the Nike swoosh!'

'Hey, that seems confusing. Brands cost more than

the actual same commodity. So, a no-name toothpaste, or a shop-brand toothpaste is much cheaper than Colgate. The company makes extra profits because of the brand name. Why should consumers like brands? Seems counter-intuitive.'

'The simple truth as to why brands will survive is that consumers love brands. They serve consumers well, who then make common cause with brands. They save consumers valuable time and effort. They offer a standard of quality, reliability and trust. And in the case of some product brands, they stand for snob appeal. Like your new S-Class Mercedes, Shankar!'

'No. Mine is a C-Class, my friend. You drive an E-Class I am told,' said Shankar with a smirk.

'Not yet, sir. But coming to branding, this is not the first time that big packaged goods brands have come under attack. In the 1960s, supermarket chains were trying to push their own brands in the UK, just as they are trying to do in India now. Then too, there were doomsday predictions that big packaged brands would vanish as modestly priced, good-quality house brands were made available in supermarkets like Tesco. House brands did not kill big packaged goods brands, though they may have dented their profit margin. In the US, P&G created the "Everyday Low Prices" campaign in partnership with Walmart and that slowed down house brands. Let us be clear, big brands are here to stay because not only are manufacturers dependent on them to make the extra profit, but consumers love them for the promise they make and keep every time they buy a brand they know and trust.'

Shankar was quiet for a bit, letting what I had said sink in. I sensed that he would come back to me with another question. And he did, pretty soon. 'So tell me, does branding matter for a company like mine? I know my customers. They know me. I get good references. And my business is growing. What does branding have to do with my kind of business-to-business operation?'

'Shankar, in a sense every company is a brand. For instance, let us assume ABC Cola company had a stock market value of around $100 billion. Yet, its book value, that is the net asset value, may be only $10 billion. A vast part of the valuation of the business comes from the brand, or the reputation. Similarly, if your company had a market cap of Rs 2,000 crores and your net assets are valued at Rs 1,500 crores, then your brand value is Rs 500 crores. I am making it too simplistic, but you get the picture, right? All businesses are brands. You can call it goodwill or reputation or brand value. Same thing really. And this value can go up and down.'

'But will I get more business if my brand is better known? I am not sure.'

'Well, it depends. If I replace the word "brand" with the word "reputation", then you'll probably agree with me in a flash. A better reputation will definitely get you more enquiries. For instance, you are the best-known brand in gaskets. So, people call you first. A smaller company may also get called and you may have to compete with them on all kinds of parameters. But for now, you get that first call. So, a better brand has higher recall and gets invited first.

Once the first step is done, the better brand always has better bargaining power. If you play it right, you can command a better price. A buyer may be willing to give you more for your product. In addition, they may also give you better terms. Obviously, you cannot get away with ridiculous terms. But a better brand gets better treatment from the buyer. If you remember, there used to be an expression in the world of computers—"Nobody ever got fired for buying IBM". Now, once you get the order and you are able to match the quality, a better brand will often get you better loyalty. In short, a better corporate reputation and a better brand has several positive spin-offs.'

'Okay, tell me more ... what else can a good corporate brand do for someone like me?' asked Shankar.

'Yeah, sure. So, we just talked about better leverage with your principals, that is, the companies who buy from you. But that is not all. For example, a company with a better brand name attracts better talent. Tell me, after your company had that terrific IPO and glowing reports in the media, did you see a dramatic improvement in the quality of job applications and the CVs you received?'

'Yes, now that you say it, I did get some calls that I wasn't getting before the IPO. So, maybe the IPO improved our brand image, is it?' Shankar was beginning to accept that some of my arguments about the benefits of branding were working for him too.

'Definitely! I remember the time when TCS was seen as losing ground to Infosys. That changed the day the TCS stock was listed in the stock exchange. And now they are a darling of the stock markets.'

Shankar thought for a bit, 'Ah, I get it, you must have handled the IPO advertising of TCS. Arré yaar, don't keep selling to me. So, according to you, branding as a concept is not too new, but not as old as marketing. To me it seems like it has taken some time to travel from FMCG companies to other sectors. But can everything be branded?'

'Shankar, as far as marketing literature is concerned, branding as a concept has been studied deeply only in the last fifty years. But it has existed for far longer than that. We see it all around us. To the extent that sometimes it is unwelcome, and even despised.'

'Despised? How is that possible?' asked Shankar.

'Hmm, let me think of an example for you. Have you heard of Adele? She's a pop music sensation.'

'Yes, I think my kids are big fans of hers.'

'I'm sure they are. She's been ragingly popular since her first album, *19*, was released. All her albums so far have been titled after her age when she started working on them—*19, 21, 25*—that's her latest one. Anyway, she is such a big star and she hates being called a brand. In an interview she said that she hated the word and it made her sound like a fabric softener or a pack of chips.'

Shankar had forgotten his original question about selling dreams and was now getting deeper and deeper into the world of branding. And I was on surer ground.

'Tell me, can anything become a brand?'

'Almost everything, yes. We are surrounded by brands. IPL is a sports brand. WWF is a not-for-profit brand. Adele is a brand, whether she likes it or not. Anand Mahindra is a brand. As are you.'

'Me? A brand? Not possible, yaar! I am a simple small-town guy who had a dream. And I am still a small-town guy at heart.'

I paused for a moment. Shankar hailed from a small town in Gujarat. His father ran a business selling auto parts in that town. It was gratifying to see that Shankar had not let the IPO, the wealth and the accolades go to his head. I had heard that he had quietly been doing a lot of CSR work in his hometown—a new school, a hospital, a motor training school and even an automobile mechanic training institute. He was probably a big celebrity in that town.

'Yes, you are quite a brand, Shankar. And you can learn how to keep building your personal brand. For yourself, as well as for the sake of your company,' I added.

'I can understand I need a brand for my ego. But why does my company need my personal brand?' Shankar was curious.

'Let me use an example again. I got an interesting insight into family-managed businesses a few months ago at a conference. It was a panel with four managing directors of family-managed companies. I am not saying that yours is a family-managed company, but one of the panelists narrated an interesting story. She said that her father had told her that in the early stages of their business, once the initial struggle was over, the company was there to provide for the family. It gave them wealth, security and comfort. But after a period of time, after the company has achieved a level of success and was run by a blended team of professionals and family, the family has to be there for the company. She said that her father had told them that they need to be alert, vigilant and also build their own personal brand, because it would help the company's progress,' I said summing up the argument.

We slowed down to absorb the serenity around us. The quietude, the night sky gently reflecting on the lakes around us, wild grass asleep in the cool darkness.

We had reached the IIMC 'Howrah Bridge'. It is a small bridge going over lakes numbered three and four. We spotted a couple on the bridge, in deep conversation.

2

Am I a Brand?

AS WE APPROACHED IIMC'S OWN LITTLE HOWRAH Bridge, we realised that the couple in deep conversation were none other than Rita Singh and Kunal Sharma. They, too, were our batchmates and were on campus for the reunion.

Rita was a rare person in our class of two hundred students. She was a BA in psychology amidst a sea of engineers. From the day she entered the wonderful Joka campus, she was clear that she wanted to work in human resources. She did struggle with some of our subjects, especially financial accounting and the compulsory statistics and numerical analysis, but she persisted and managed to keep her head above water. And she shone in subjects like economics and behavioural sciences, often getting into debates with our professors on the complexities of macroeconomics and GDP measurements. She was always in top form during organisational behaviour classes. She would read scholarly articles from academic journals and engage the professors in long-winded arguments on how to manage the psychology and motivation of employees. Some students used to call her Revolver Rita since her questions were often zingers.

Kunal Sharma, her husband of twenty-three years, was also from our class. An engineer with great proficiency in complex numerical analysis, he majored in finance. His first job was with a multinational bank where he spent almost a decade, rising rapidly across multiple departments. He then joined an Indian financial services firm that advised companies on mergers and acquisitions. He became a senior partner within a few years, managing several key client relationships. Rita and Kunal lived in Mumbai and, unlike Shankar, they were in regular touch with me.

'Hey guys, apologies for interrupting your romantic moment. Please just ignore us,' I shouted as we started to quickly navigate the narrow Howrah Bridge.

'What romance are you talking about? We were discussing our daughter's education plans. All suggestions are welcome,' Rita said.

Shankar and I stopped to chat with Rita and Kunal. 'We are no experts on higher education, Rita, but I know that graduate studies in the US is indeed in a different league. Though I am saying this standing on IIMC's haloed grounds and totally run the risk of IIMC withdrawing my diploma,' said Shankar laughing. His son was hoping to get into one of the top business schools in the US and I realised that this was an answer from a father who had done a fair bit of research. Truth be told, it is probably easier to get into a top school in the US than to get into IIMC, but Shankar wasn't about to admit that.

'Yeah man, there are so many more options now than there were in our time. Anyway, what are you two discussing so seriously?' asked Kunal.

'Oh, Ambi is telling me about the wonderful world of branding. And all I had asked him, to start with, was about dreams!' said Shankar.

'Branding? Well, that's an interesting topic. Would you mind if we join you on your branding walk?' asked Rita. Kunal looked at Rita and nodded; maybe he wanted to say no but, knowing Rita, he had little choice.

On our part, we were happy to have some interesting company. I was getting tired of my monologues and was ready for other perspectives. We got off the bridge and continued our slow walk.

Kunal was the one who posed the first question, 'So Ambi, what is the simplest definition of a brand that you have come across?'

I wasn't sure if Kunal was testing me but I played along. 'Well, simply put, a brand is a name that tells a story,' I said.

'Aah, finally he is going to tell us about selling dreams,' chimed in Shankar.

'Well, Shankar, more than just dreams, a brand has to tell a story to its consumers so that they will remember the name when they go out to shop. For instance, when I say Lux, does a story come to your mind?'

'A lovely film star in a bath tub,' said Shankar.

'Exactly. So, a soap that is a favourite of film stars. Now if I say Amul, what comes to mind?'

'Well, milk and a great co-operative movement and good value products,' said Rita.

'Right. The fact that most people know that Amul is owned by farmers is not an accident. The company actually funded the production of a film....'

'*Manthan?*' asked Kunal.

'Yes, *Manthan.* The film tells the story of how Amul was born. Our children's generation may not have heard of *Manthan*, but Amul doesn't fail to remind its customers that all the money they pay goes to the dairy farmer.'

'That's true, Amul is indeed a name with a great story,' Rita added.

'Not just Amul, several major corporate names have stories behind them. Look at Tata. The stories behind Tata Steel and Taj Hotels are legendary. Tata's philanthropic activities, such as the Indian Institute of Science, Tata Institute of Social Sciences (TISS), Tata Institute of Fundamental Research and Tata Cancer Hospitals, are all well known.'

Rita was quick to add, 'I know TISS produces some of the best HR professionals in the country. And even in IIMC we have a Tata Hall.'

'Coming to smaller brands, they all have a story to tell. Take Santoor. It tells the story of a mom being mistaken for someone younger. Fevicol is about the unbreakable bond and Parachute is about the purity of coconut oil. All these are names that tell stories,' I concluded my discourse.

Coincidentally, we had reached Tata Hall, the old Management Development Centre at IIMC that was supported by the Tata Group some decades ago. Tata Hall was not used much nowadays since the new MDC had come up. But for some of us old-timers, it still held its charm, with its old rooms and a canteen run by the trusted Mihir-da. His *macher jhol* was to die for.

'Rita, I was telling Shankar that people are brands too. Mihir-da is a brand. Shankar is also a brand. You are an HR expert. What is your opinion about this observation of mine?' I wanted to get a psychologist's view on this and bring Rita into the conversation.

Rita was quick to respond, 'I totally agree that every executive is a brand. Some executives realise this early on in their career, some realise it late. These days universities are advising students to make sure their online presence is clean. Many prospective employers these days do an online search on a candidate before shortlisting. Now, we even have companies that do this for a fee. So let alone film stars, politicians, athletes or CEOs, even a mid-level executive is a brand in some sense.'

Rita had brought up a really interesting trend. 'I am reminded of a story that I have heard, though I don't know how true this is. A business school, government run I think, was looking to hire a new director. The interview panel consisted of three eminent old men. They met five candidates after going through their CVs that were submitted to the selection team in Delhi. The panel finalised one of those candidates. Excellent academic record, great education, just the right experience, and so on. One of the interviewers, on his way to the airport, decided to Google the selected candidate's name. And among the top five search results was a news report of a sexual misconduct committed by that person. I am telling you a story that goes back some ten years. But it was shocking that the selection team had not done its due diligence before shortlisting the candidates,' I added.

'So what happened?' Kunal was curious.

'Fortunately, the paperwork had not been done and the panel decided to go with the next-in-line candidate who was equally good, and with a blemish-free Google reputation to boot,' I laughed as I narrated that story.

'So true. Today, a reputation, or your personal brand, needs to be built across all fronts,' added Rita.

'Ambi tells me that I am a brand and I had no idea. But if you were to advice my managers to become brands, where will you start Rita?' asked Shankar.

'I guess it will have to start with the realisation that there is a brand called "You". You work for this brand and then you work for a company called Perfect Gaskets founded by a team of engineers. These need to go together. The next step is to figure out what is your brand. How will you define your personal brand? Which market do you cater to? And how are you keeping your brand story going?' Rita replied.

'That is too much for us to grasp, Ms Revolver. Can you explain that in a simple profit and loss format?' Kunal bowled a googly to his wife.

I deflected that googly, 'Personal branding is a difficult topic to get your handle on. You can question, why should my senior managers have a brand of their own, they are representing the company, which is a strong brand anyway. And that is partly true. But understanding the importance of personal branding can help your team get even better at their jobs.'

'Yes, that's so true. Personal branding needs to start with where your brand is at the moment. Who does your personal brand matter to? For instance, if I am the CFO of, say, a company like Perfect Gaskets, what should my brand stand for? Who is my target audience or market? Maybe my bankers, or CFOs of my customer organisations. Definitely my own team. My peers in the company and the board, maybe. What should be the story my brand should tell them?' Rita painted a nice picture.

'Yes, my CFO also needs to address the investors and the media, now that we are a public company. But does personal branding matter to the other not-so-senior managers?' asked Shankar.

Rita continued, 'Definitely. I think everyone at the mid to senior level in any organisation has to realise that they are a brand. And then figure out how they want to present their brand, and how to keep refreshing their brand story.'

Lost in conversation, the four of us hadn't realised that we had reached Ramanujam Hall, which had been a hostel in our days at the campus. We decided to go in and have some tea. We resisted the temptation of visiting our old rooms. The tea break lasted a full fifteen minutes. Piping hot Maggi was also on offer and reminded us of our days on campus. There were a few students still around and our guess was that the tea shop was catering to them, in the absence of a full-fledged dining facilty during the December break. Temptation was put on a tight leash—no Maggi for now!

Our tea break ended with Shankar saying, 'I am not sure of this at all. This personal branding stuff is nonsense.' Looked like we had more important topics to discuss than tea or Maggi.

3

Isn't There a Dichotomy?

'HOW CAN A COMPANY ENCOURAGE EVERYONE TO BUILD their personal brand? It will lead to mayhem,' Shankar asked quite belligerently.

I thought he had a point. If you encourage all your mid-level managers to go about building their own personal brands, then they may end up sending out mixed messages in the market, confusing everyone. And it maybe confusing for them too. But at the same time, if a company's employees work in a nameless, featureless way, that has its own problems. There are exceptions in the world of media. While *The New York Times* has some great columnists, like Thomas Friedman and Maureen Dowd, whose personal branding is on point, *The Economist* does not promote any bylines for its writers. And both publications are equally renowned and well-respected for their world-class journalism.

So, Shankar's concern was valid. But there had to be an answer.

'Well, imagine the opposite, Shankar. If in your company no one is aware of the power of personal branding and they all blindly toe the corporate line, where will that lead you? You might end up becoming a boring company full of robots,' I commented.

Rita was quick to add, 'Whether you like it or not, today's executives—junior and senior—are spending time and effort polishing their personal brand. I run an HR consultancy now and I do a fair bit of executive coaching. I am yet to meet a senior or middle-level manager who is not keen on understanding the power of personal branding.'

'Arré, but will that not hurt the overall corporate message and reputation?' Shankar was unconvinced.

'Yes, if you are not careful, your executives may start building their personal brand in diverse directions that might end up marring the company they work for. For example, if some of your executives start advocating against the use of cars, it can harm your company. But for such exceptions, it is to the strength of the company if there are powerful personal brands working under its umbrella,' Rita added.

'What are the benefits for the company if it has powerful personal brands working for it? I just don't see the connection,' Shankar persisted.

Kunal, who had been listening to the discussion silently all this while, finally spoke. 'Shankar, I work in the financial services sector. In our sector the firm's brand is the most important, but each of our partners have to have a strong brand aura too. And even our client services directors, yet to become partners, are actively building their personal brand. We encourage it since this helps us in three simple ways. One, potential clients want to work with people who have a powerful aura. They believe that even if the firm is providing the overall business, tools and techniques, the individual can bring in or take away a lot from the overall deal. Secondly, the best talent in the company wants to work with the most powerful personal brand. In a firm like ours, with around two hundred highly qualified MBAs, CAs, MScs and PhDs, it is always a challenge to get a project team going. A team leader with a powerful personal brand helps rally the troops. Thirdly, having a powerful brand helps in building relationships with your ecosystem. Be it the media, the government authorities, industry bodies, and so on. Our firm has a policy in place to encourage our senior and mid-level managers to develop their personal brands. In fact, we had invited Ambi to speak to our team on the importance of building a personal brand. I know that this may not squarely apply to a manufacturing set-up like yours, but at least in professional services firms, building a personal brand is a must.'

Kunal's input was really helpful and I took it further, 'Kunal, you've explained that so cogently, but don't dismiss the importance of personal branding in a manufacturing set-up. I remember listening to the head of manufacturing of an automobile major at a Confederation of Indian Industry (CII) seminar on building excellence. I was so impressed with that guy and he made great sense.'

'Arré, what exactly did he say?' Shankar wanted to know.

'Shankar, he was from a giant company. They wanted to get everyone in their company, in any supervisory capacity, to understand a car buyer, what does she look for, how does she go about buying a car, what makes them go from a maybe to a yes. So they started a programme called "each one sell one". Every one of their supervisor-level people across departments, from the shop floor to supply chain and even development, had to spend a day in a dealership and sell a car. And this exercise had a profound impact on the people in the company. I was totally impressed. Both with the story and the person who narrated it,' I added.

Shankar was listening and even nodding in agreement to what Kunal and I were saying. It looked like the car company story had made an impact on him and I could imagine him thinking if someone in his team would be able to tell a story like that.

Our group of four had almost stopped walking, given the animated discussion we were involved in. We did not realise that we were standing in front of the auditorium. This was built after our time and could seat over seven hundred people. The annual convocation used to be held in this auditorium for many years, till the batch size swelled to four hundred. So, with students, their families and the campus staff, the convocations now have some 1,500 attendees, and the institute has had to create large, temporary, air-conditioned facilities to host the convocation, which is usually held in the scorching heat of April.

'But tell me, how does a company like mine navigate the dichotomy of corporate branding and personal branding?' Shankar asked in a more mollified tone.

'All companies are brands, that you agree, right Shankar? So now your question is, why should a manufacturing company, such as yours, encourage the personal branding efforts of its employees?' Rita asked.

'Yes, exactly. I am still not sure,' Shankar added.

'Even in an engineering company there will be executives who want to build their personal brand. Some of them may be doing it to ensure that they can get a better job. But, in my experience, many of them are doing it to do better in their current job. Irrespective of the company they work in. By becoming a stronger, focused personal brand, they get better recognition in the company, they get invited to various forums within the company and they are also able to motivate their teams better. I should add that the HR team needs to keep an eye on whose personal brand could be detrimental to the company. For example, should one of your senior executives speak in a seminar where the other speakers are dubious? Or should your executives be allowed to enter an award show where the nominees have to pay a fee?' Rita expounded.

'What?! An award that you have pay for?' asked Kunal.

Rita smirked, 'Yup, I can get you the Best CFO of the Year award. You just have to cough up a few lakh rupees.'

That statement from Rita stunned Kunal and Shankar into total silence. We were all thinking about the many emails we get from friends and professional contacts announcing their awards.

'Is that really true?' Shankar wanted to make sure.

'Yes, yes, Shankar. There is an entire award industry that

has sprung up to support the personal branding efforts of mid-level executives. CHRO of the year. CMO of the year. The most powerful supply chain manager. The internal auditor of the year. You name it, there is an award for it,' I added.

Rita did not want the discussion to digress into trivial award hunger. 'As I was saying,' Rita concluded her argument, 'the HR department has to keep an eye on the personal brand building efforts of the executives. If someone is going out of line or doing something that can hurt the company, then the HR department needs to tell them to lay off. If someone takes a political or religious stance that is not in line with the corporate policy, they would need to be reined in.'

'I get it. Even for an engineering company I need to encourage personal branding efforts. And I should not see it as executives trying to build their resume. But tell me, is there a process to it that we can advise our people about?' Shankar posed his next question.

We had been sitting on the nicely manicured lawns in front of the auditorium. Suddenly we realised that our clothes were getting wet. The night dew that was forming on the grass was now building its personal brand on our trousers. It was time to resume our walk.

4

Where Do You Start?

THE FOUR OF US GOT UP IN A HURRY AND EXAMINED our trousers. We were relieved to see that it was not a Mayday situation, and began walking again.

Shankar was beginning to get off the fence, 'Okay guys, I agree that personal branding may be applicable across industries, not just the services sector. Even in a business-to-business manufacturing set-up like mine, there is ample scope for personal branding. But where do you start the journey?'

'The way you start the branding journey for any product, Shankar,' I replied.

'Well, with a product you start with the name and the packaging, right?' asked Shankar.

'Yes. When it comes to personal branding you already have your name given to you by your parents,' I began, but was interrupted by Rita.

'I know of some people who have opted to truncate their name or ask their friends and colleagues to call them by a new name. Say your name is Meyaiappan, you may want to ask your friends to call you Maps. I know of an Alagappan who was called Alex. One of the founders of Infosys, Senapathy Gopalakrishnan officially writes his name as Kris Gopalakrishnan. This is a practical step since international clients may find it difficult to pronounce Gopalakrishnan.'

'Interesting examples, Rita. So just as a brand starts with a brand name, you too start with a name. The next step in personal branding is called impression management. And when it comes to impressions, the first step is really your appearance, how you present yourself. When I started working in advertising, I decided to grow a beard. Many of my seniors had beards and I thought a beard would make me look very intellectual. But when I joined a British multinational ...'

'You went to work with Boots, right?' It was Shankar who interrupted me this time.

'Yes, Boots. My credentials were good and I had good references, but I did not look the British MNC type. So, one day, I ran into the MD of the company in the washroom and he commented, "Mr Ambi, a beard may be okay for advertising. But we are a British healthcare pharma multinational ..." He did not ask me to remove my beard, but I got the message. And these little nuances are quite dynamic. I am talking of things that happened twenty years ago. Back then, a beard was okay for the creative industries, but not so much in other sectors. Today, a beard is not just okay, it's quite fashionable to sport one. Twenty years ago, none of the cricketers of the Indian team had a beard.

Today most of them do, including the captain,' I concluded.

'You shaved your beard. But have you heard of a world leader who grew a beard because he took an eleven-year-old's advice to heart?' asked Rita.

'Really? Arré, who are you talking about?' Shankar was intrigued.

'This is a true story. Abraham Lincoln received a letter from a eleven-year-old girl before he won the American presidential election. In that letter the little girl asked him to grow whiskers, saying that would help her convince her older brothers to vote for him. Abraham Lincoln thanked her in his reply. He won the election and later took her advice to grow a beard, or whiskers as the little girl mentioned. If you look up Lincoln, you will mostly find pictures of him with a beard. But you can sometimes spot a rare picture of him clean-shaven. Maybe he was destined to enter the history books with a beard. It was the Lincoln with a beard who enacted the abolishment of slavery which led to the civil war. It was also that Lincoln who delivered "The Gettysburg Address".

'Impression management starts with personal appearance, definitely. Some corporate HR teams even have an orientation for their new recruits on what the company expects in the personal appearance department. Grooming is also something that some of our executives need to learn about,' Rita concluded her argument.

'I think that grooming and personal appearance issues have become more important now that we can see such a heartening diversity in young employees. I remember interviewing a guy from a top school. He was really bright but ill-at-ease in poorly fitted clothes. It turned out that he had borrowed his father's wedding suit—the only suit he could get hold of,' added Kunal.

'Yaar, even I had only one suit for many years after IIM. The same one I got made for placement,' chimed in Shankar.

'And today you can buy a shop or even a suiting manufacturing company,' Kunal piped in.

Rita added an interesting example to not overstate the importance of personal appearance. 'Guys, I have a friend who is the HR head at a London-based financial firm. A few years back, she recruited some top-class analytical guys from India's best engineering colleges. These guys were all toppers, but a bit clueless about dressing to impress. They arrived in London with identical black backpacks. The British office assistants called them "the paratroopers from India". My friend wondered if her new recruits would fit in. Soon enough the paratroopers from India managed to prove the hiring decision right by delivering way beyond expectations at work. The company then decided to hire regularly from India.'

'Of course, the quality of your work is paramount. But as far as impression management goes, the next consideration are your manners. These could consist of gestures, facial expressions, body language and your language. I truly believe that the rise of women in corporate hierarchy has had a beneficial effect on how men behave, on their impression management. For instance, with senior women executives around, the boardroom language has become a lot more polite and gentlemanly,' I added.

'So the rise of women has helped improve the impression men make. That is a terrible backhanded compliment, I think,' the Revolver fired a shot at me.

'Arré, all this seems too simple to me. You need to be well-dressed. You should be well-groomed. You need to be polite,' Shankar added incredulously. 'But surely this is all quite basic. Is that all there is to this brouhaha about personal branding?'

'This is just the first step, Shankar. There are a total of three steps,' I added. 'The second step is a little more complex. This involves the personal brand identity you want to project. What capital do you bring to a relationship—competency capital or relationship capital?'

'Ambi, are you speaking about what a person needs to emphasise? Whether one is going to emphasise competence or relationship or a combination of both?' Rita asked.

'Yes, Rita. Competency capital is about your knowledge and skills. For example, if you are in marketing, how competent are you in that field. And you build your personal brand around competency capital. The other capital is what is called relationship capital. This emphasises your ability to build social connections. I know that to be professionally successful you need to have both. You cannot just be a relationships person, or be just a subject matter expert with no social skills. And there are people in every company who fall into these two buckets. Can you think of some examples in your company, Shankar?' I asked.

'Interesting. We were three of us who started this company. I was always seen as the technical wizard. So, I suppose I focused on my competency capital. One of my partners, also an engineer, is great at meeting clients and building relationships with the employees. So, he is probably the relationship capital guy. My third partner is good at both. So, he is probably the only balanced brand,' Shankar observed wisely.

'So, the first step is impression management. The second is identity management. Both sound interesting. What is the third step? Is it your ability to navigate between the two?' asked Kunal.

'In personal brand management principles, we call it reflexivity. In simple terms, it is about how good you are in reflecting on your personal brand image. Are you in control of your personal brand? Are you aware of how your personal brand is being projected on those around you? There are two aspects to this step. Firstly, whenever you say or do something, you need to understand how it is being received. This is called reflection in action. You may say something with a certain intention or meaning, but it may be received differently. There is an old paradigm in advertising—perception is reality. So, you need to be able to gauge the receiver's reaction to what you are saying or doing. The second is even more interesting. It is called reflection on action. What you say or do is seen differently by your audience because of your personal aura. So, the same thing said by someone else may be received differently. Yeh sab personal brand ki maya hai,' I concluded.

'I get it. Make a good first impression—dress well, speak well, and shave, Ambi. Then figure out what you want to focus on—competence or relationship. Ideally, both in balance. The third step is to reflect on your branding strategy. Understand how it is impacting what you are saying, doing, etc.', Shankar summarised our discussion.

Shankar was really trying to grasp the whole process of personal brand building, but perhaps I had made it too simplistic by breaking it down into three steps.

'Indeed, those are the nuts and bolts of the entire personal branding process. But there are many, many layers to it. It is about telling your unique story through your appearance, mannerisms, presentation, words, letters, tweets, quirks, etc. You need to possess three key criteria—clarity, consistency and constancy. You need to be clear what you want to be, what you want to project. You need to be consistent in what you are saying and doing. And you need to be in tune with the times, constantly,' I added.

'So Ambi, tell us how does a young manager start on his personal branding journey?' Kunal asked the next poser.

5

Is There a Journey Map?

'OH, OH, KUNAL HOLD IT. FIRST, I WANT TO KNOW IF these personal branding steps are applicable only to the seniors in the company or to everyone,' Shankar added on to what Kunal had asked.

'You tell me, Shankar. You have so many bright people working with you. Name three of them and let us see if they are coming through as impressive personal brands,' Rita chimed in.

'Hmmm, let me think. There is this girl in marketing called Ankita. She is very bright and often helps me with the presentations that I am forced to make for industry forums. Then there is Paritosh in finance. He is a deep, strategic thinker and way more mature than his thirty-two years of age. I often send complex problems to him and he is ready with a coherent strategy in a few days. And the third is Rajagopal in operations. He has created some terrific models to help us rationalise our inventory cycles,' said Shankar, answering Rita's question.

'You're a lucky boss. Do you think these three people have built their personal brand well?' asked Kunal.

I answered instead of Shankar, 'Since the MD and founder of a large company like Perfect Gaskets remembers their names and what they do, they must be doing something right. I do not know if they have built their brand consciously or if it was all happenstance. Or maybe they are practising the eleven-question journey of personal brand building.'

'What eleven questions?' Shankar was quick to pounce.

'Well, you can call them ten or eleven questions. But let us first admit that you cannot build your personal brand if you are incompetent or have very poor emotional quotient (EQ). The personal branding journey starts with what you see as your career. What is the destination you are heading towards?

'Then you need to visualise yourself five, ten, fifteen years down the line. What will you be doing? Where will you be? As you do this, you need to assess your loyalties. How loyal are you to yourself, how loyal are you to your company, how loyal are you to your immediate boss,' I said.

'Speaking of loyalty, Ambi, is it true that in advertising, teams move together from agency to agency?' Rita asked.

'That is also true of the merchant banking business, Rita. I suppose this is true of most industries today, be it hospitality, travel, media, etc. I suppose this is a part of not managing individual aspirations with corporate aspirations. The ordinate and superordinate goals, so to speak,' added Kunal.

'Arré baba, now what is this ordinate and superordinate goals stuff, Kunal?' Shankar looked confounded.

'Ordinate goals are your own. Superordinate goals are goals that may not be in line with yours, but are needed for the long-term success of the company. So, you may hate living in Delhi, but you have to take charge of the Delhi office and run it for three years because your company needs you to do that,' Kunal explained.

'So, when you are planning your personal branding journey, you need to be aware that in order to build a long-term career you may need to make some short-term sacrifices. The most important step in the personal branding journey is to figure out, as early as you can, what what your authentic self is. What is your point of difference. You cannot be something you are not happy being,' I added.

'Then you need to develop a narrative of your personal brand. What will it look like, how will it sound? It looks like Ankita, Paritosh and Rajagopal have done a great job. You were able to describe them to us in a simple yet cogent manner. Here you can also learn from the big visible brands and how they go about diligently building their brand aura. You need to keep reintroducing yourself to people and not take your brand for granted. And, of course, you need to prove your worth all the time. Be consistent in what you do. Balance the two things we spoke about earlier.'

'I know, I know, competence capital and relationship capital,' Shankar chimed in.

'Yes. In other words, you need to balance domain knowledge with social relationship management. You need to build and manage your networks. Figure out how to be more influential, seek and humbly accept feedback,' I continued.

'Interesting! All the three young managers I mentioned insist that I give them feedback after every session I have with them. Sometimes I tell them what they did was fine. And they often insist that they need to know what they can do better,' said Shankar.

Kunal nodded in agreement, 'Today's youngsters want bosses who give consistent and constructive feedback. I had to counsel one of my partners because I heard he was being too diplomatic with his feedback. And this was being noticed. His project team members felt that they were not learning enough by working with him. Young employees need a balance of criticism and praise. You do too little of one and too much of the other, they desert the ship.'

Rita had been listening to us for a while, and finally spoke up, 'Kunal, that's a very valid point. Gone are the days when people worked in one job in one company for years and years. I see the emergence of "projectisation" of work. Young people want to work on new projects every few years, if not months. They find that they can learn so much more as they move from project to project.'

'Very true, Rita. Youngsters are clear that feedback is important since the final question is about reassessing where you stand. People today want to figure out what they are good at, what they like doing and what will make them authentic. They then want to polish their skills, build an identity, and become more visible. They want to communicate with the right target audience, balancing style with substance; they want to build their networks, learn to influence, seek feedback and reassess their progress all the time. There, those are the various stages of personal brand building. And these steps apply to all levels of an organisation,' I concluded.

Stages of Personal Brand Building

What are you good at?	How to become more visible?
What do you like doing?	How to communicate with the right target audience?
What will make you authentic?	How to balance style and substance?
How to polish your skills?	How to build a network?
How to build your identity?	How to influence?

To this Rita responded, 'Interesting that you listed ten questions. I often use just three when I'm coaching executives. The first question is: what differentiates you from all the others of the same background or experience. The second question is: what value can you create for others, be it as a colleague, boss, friend or subordinate. The final question is: in what you do, what is it that makes you feel satisfied and fulfilled.'

'What you are saying is so true. My three employees that I spoke about always appear happy with their work. Sometimes I wonder if I am overburdening them, but they're always up for new challenges,' Shankar said.

'Shankar, chances are that in their own way they are practising the process we spoke about. They have extracted their unique proposition. They are doing a good job of expressing it in their own ways. The next thing they have to do is exude it, internally and externally,' I added.

Rita continued my thought, 'And Shankar, what you said is so true. The three people you spoke about are using you as a sounding board to keep improving. I suspect that they are learning from you like a sponge.'

We had completed one full circle around the campus and had come back to the MDP Centre where we had started our journey. But our conversation was far from over and we were not ready to stop. Several old friends were waving at us, asking us to join them in their room for a get together with a 'religious' friend—an Old Monk, in fact.

Shankar, Kunal and Rita waved back and told them that they were discussing more important aspects with an older monk. Since I was no longer a follower of the Monk, I was quite happy to continue our walk. And the second lap started.

Shankar was the first one off the block, 'Arré, where were we? Oh yeah, tell me Ambi, when a young person starts building her personal brand, is there a simple algorithm she can follow?'

'In branding circles, there is this concept called the brand mantra,' I said.

'From Old Monk to mantra, wah! But what is a brand mantra?' Kunal asked.

'These ad types give these clever names to simple things,' Rita's revolver shot.

I laughed. 'You can call it a gimmick, but it's an interesting one. And I think it is applicable to building a personal brand as well. Tell me the top three words that come to your mind when I say Disney. Just three, please.'

'Fun.'

'Entertainment.'

'Theme parks.'

'Cartoons.'

'Movies.'

'Musical.'

'Yes, these are all correct. But if you were to pick just three words, what would they be?' I asked again.

'Fun, entertainment, profits,' said Kunal.

'Movies, masti, magic,' said Shankar.

'Aah, Shankar, that was the tagline of the Zee Cinema channel. Our agency had done some terrific ads around that. But wrong,' I added.

'What about fun, family, entertainment?' This was Rita.

'Brilliant! So, the three-word brand mantra that reflects the brand Disney is "fun, family, entertainment". You see, each word is critical and tells you something essential about Disney. You replace any one of these words and you get a totally different meaning,' I revealed.

Kunal, the M&A expert, came in quickly with the observation, 'It will be interesting how Disney is going to handle the Fox Network content after the acquisition.'

'Yes, I think they may have to park some of the

properties under a different brand. When Disney launched its streaming platform, they had to ensure that their content was not as risqué as some of the shows on Netflix,' I observed.

'Can you think of more examples for brand mantra? I am trying to see if it can work for all brands,' asked Shankar.

'Yes, technically, you can write a brand mantra for all brands. For example, by changing just one word of Disney's brand mantra, you get McDonald's—fun, family, food. Or in the case of Nike, it is "authentic athletic performance". For a homegrown brand like say FabIndia, it could be "natural social style". This would be very different from, say, a brand like Ritu Kumar,' I tried explaining the concept.

'And do you think the concept of brand mantra is applicable even to personal branding?' Kunal asked.

I thought for a bit and before I could reply Rita jumped in, 'I think it is an interesting concept to apply to personal brands as well. There are loads of positive characteristics that a person can possess. Like analytical, creative, driven, humble, outgoing, prepared, trustworthy, inspired, honest, positive, proactive, happy, sensitive, values-driven, etc. There is of course, the famous 24 Character Strengths test that HR professionals use for evaluating candidates. What Ambi presented as brand mantra can equally apply to personal brands.'

Shankar was very invested in this whole concept. 'Interesting. So, if I am a fresh graduate and starting out in my career, then it will be worth my while to figure out the three or four words that will be used to describe me.

For instance, "independent, insightful, tireless" versus "creative, proactive, sociable" are two different brands in my view.'

'So, if you want to build your personal brand, it may be worth your while to craft a few options and speak to people around you on which of those describe you the best. It is one thing to want to be seen as sociable, but your behaviour has to reflect it. The simple test of that is whether the mantra represents you and feels true to you. Is the mantra something that will create value for you and your organisation? What are the risks of embracing this particular mantra? And can you live the brand mantra?' said Rita as a concluding argument.

'Wonderful, Rita. If a youngster wants to build her personal brand, then figuring out her brand mantra is a great place to start. As we saw earlier, it has to be genuine. You cannot sustain a brand mantra which is not authentically you. You cannot want to be seen as easy-going, when you are actually a very task-oriented person,' I added.

'I mentioned three names from my own company. I am sure they are building powerful personal brands, with or without the knowledge of the personal branding process. But I think they too can benefit from this gyan. Of course, many people can benefit from this. Maybe I too should invite Ambi for a session!' Shankar said smiling magnanimously.

'Anytime, yaar! So finally, you see that branding can work for people too. And brand building is not just about selling dreams. When building a personal brand, you need to start by defining your personal ambition, your personal vision. Then you need to define your personal brand, what is your personal SWOT,* what are your specialisations. You may even develop your personal scorecard that might consist of critical success factors, performance measures, improvement actions, just as you would if you are working on a brand of soap or toothpaste. You then need to implement your personal branding journey, and cultivate your ambition without letting it get ahead of you.' I was wanting to make an even better impression on Shankar. But maybe I was getting ahead of myself.

'Hey, hey, not so quick with the concluding remarks,' Kunal interrupted in an aggressive tone. 'What if you get stuck in what you think is the wrong brand mantra for you?'

We had walked quite a distance from the MDC and were approaching the small Nestlé shack on campus. Fortunately for us, it was still open. Rita looked playfully at her husband and said, 'To get an answer to that you need to buy us all coffee at the Nescafé Corner.'

---

*SWOT—Strength, Weakness, Opportunity, Threat

6

Can You Change Direction?

KUNAL GRACIOUSLY BOUGHT FOUR CUPS OF STEAMING hot coffee for us and the discussion drifted to talking about our batchmate who had joined Nestlé after IIMC. She went on to launch a blockbuster snack food brand and had, in fact, recently written a bestseller recounting her experiences.

Per usual, Shankar kept us on track. 'I am curious to know your answer to Kunal's question. What if you realise that your personal brand appeal is fading or not suited to you? What do you do then?' Shankar asked.

'The simplest answer lies in the question—what will you do if the brand appeal of your product or service fades? Let us say you are a brand of noodles and losing market share. What will you do? You go back to your consumers, some of whom are still with you and some who have moved on. You will find out what aspect of your brand has lost its appeal, what part still holds promise. After your research, you do what we call "repositioning" the brand. And then relaunch it with great fanfare,' I replied.

'This is easier said than done. Give me a recent example,' Kunal pressed on.

'Take Royal Enfield. In its heyday, it was one of the three bikes that ruled the Indian roads, along with Yezdi and Rajdoot. With the entry of better bikes, all three lost ground. The other two stopped production, but Royal Enfield continued and was supplying to the armed forces. Despite that the company was not able to see a future and cashflows were poor. That was when Eicher Motors bought Royal Enfield. They managed to reduce costs, dramatically improve quality and, with very little mass media advertising, managed to reposition the bike as a premium bike for serious bikers. A few years ago, the market cap of the company crossed that of Harley Davidson, the original bike lovers' bike,' I explained.

'Yes, I remember the deal. We were wondering how Eicher was going to manage a huge loss-making operation. But they managed to do a great job. And what you are saying is that repositioning or refreshed positioning was one of the key pillars of the turnaround strategy,' Kunal said.

'Great story, but that is with a product brand. What about personal brand? When and how do you look to change your personal brand?' Shankar asked.

'Shankar, in HR circles we look at the fit between a person and a company. So, if you are a young executive, you may have a desired personal brand image that you want to project. This might not always be in sync with your existing brand image. Add to this the company brand image. All of these might not fit together and you may be in for some confusion and change,' Rita answered.

'Exactly. When I was in advertising, my personal appearance was different. But when I joined Boots, I had to change to fit in. In my case two or three parameters changed. I went from a largely creative industry to one dominated by medical science and regulation. Secondly, I went from an Indian-owned entrepreneurial organisation to a multinational. Those who have worked in both types of organisations will have stories to tell. Thirdly, it was a British multinational, with its suit-boot culture and tea served on frilly trays,' I added.

Shankar burst out laughing and almost spilled his coffee. He recovered to add, 'Yes, I remember those days when you had a liveried waiter serving coffee and tea on fancy trays. With the teapot covered by a tea cosy.'

'How propah!' remarked Kunal. 'So, if your personal brand fits poorly with that of your company's, what do you do?'

'You can quit. Or you can redefine your personal brand, like I did. I know this can be difficult, especially when you switch between industries in two different domains. But I did manage to go from a bearded, fast-talking, rule-breaker to a tie-wearing, analytical brand manager. I could not change my stubborn nature, but that did not hurt me, since I was pretty good at the analytical part of my job.'

'Terrific. So you can alter your personal brand depending on the company you're working for. As long as you don't have to totally give up on your core identity,' Kunal observed wisely.

'In my HR practice, I spend a lot of time counselling

candidates about their brand fit. And candidates with sharp antennae are able to make changes to their personal brand. I would call the first hundred days as the critical period.'

'I shaved my beard off in less than ten days!' I had interrupted Rita, who had more to add.

'So, Ambi, you understood the need to change your personal brand ever so slightly. I am sure you had a good mentor in your new company who advised you on what to do and what not to do. I find executives at sea in a new setting. They have spent ten years of their career polishing their personal brand to fit a certain company's image, and in a new job they find that they need to abandon or alter parts of that brand identity. It can be quite obscure and unsettling. Those who have a good mentor or a coach, survive. A friend of mine is an executive coach who does what we call transition coaching, but from the employee's side,' Rita added.

'So, does personal brand reinvention only apply to people who change jobs?' Shankar asked.

'Not really, Shankar. Modern organisations are changing rapidly. There is this digital transformation of companies that is happening as we speak. So even if you are in the same organisation, you will need to constantly re-evaluate your personal brand as the company evolves. I am told executives often get caught in what is called "immunity to change". I am sure Rita knows more about this,' I said.

'Well, we are all resistant to change. When I encounter executives who are stuck in the inertial phase of change, I ask them to go through five specific steps. First, they have to realise what change they want to make. Second, they need to identify behaviour that is working against the change. Third, they need to see what is at risk because of their current behaviour. Fourth, they have to identify the barriers that are working against their change agenda. Finally, they need to identify new behaviour, may be tiny ones, that can push them towards change, For example, if you want to get fit, you have to realise that your sweet tooth will need to be controlled, you have to start by avoiding the dessert counter,' Rita added.

'Goodness! Arré, that was too much for me to digest so late at night,' Shankar shot back.

'Simply put, all successful executives are contained by their habits. Some of those habits are ingrained and resistant to change. Remember twenty years ago many senior managers used to get their emails printed out by their secretaries. They were so used to paper mail and, by refusing to adapt to email, were immune to change till such a day that they had to accept digital technology,' I supported Rita's argument.

'I have another story,' I continued. 'I once heard the managing director of a company—I think his name was Raj—who was being coached by one of the most respected CEO coaches in the country narrate this story at a conference. He said that he had attended numerous board meetings of his company as the COO. The company board and promoters then decided to promote him to the position of a managing director. He was no longer an invitee but a member of the board. He called his coach to share the good news. His coach asked him when was the first board meeting scheduled, where he would attend as MD. The board meeting was scheduled for the following week. The coach asked Raj what was going to be different. Raj could not answer. Fortunately, Raj had a terrific coach who explained that moving from a COO to an MD position was a big deal. And this would mean he had to change the way he behaved in the board meeting. Raj candidly admitted that his coach told him to enter the board meeting without any papers in his hands. "No paper, no files?" Raj told us that the coach's advice had stunned him. "Yes, no paper, no files. You have enough assistants to bring them to you," he was told. The coach also told him not to address the board members as sir or ma'am. "How do they address each other, by first name?" he was asked. When he replied in the affirmative, he was told, "So, you too will address them by their first names." Raj had told his audience how he had received many such valuable tips from his coach.

'I am recounting this story to underline the fact that the personal branding parameters of a senior executive needs to be calibrated to the position they occupy,' I ended my monologue.

Rita added, 'Let us take some of your own young and successful executives, Shankar. They may need to change too, in order to remain relevant. They will have to upgrade their skills, definitely. But more importantly they may need to change their personal brand image. Even if you work in the same company, you may need to change your personal brand because your job profile may change, your immediate boss may change or the company may be changing. And in line with this, you may have to keep refreshing your personal brand. I don't know if I am making sense.'

'In short, you need to define your destination, leverage your points of difference, develop a narrative, reintroduce yourself to your friends and colleagues, and finally, prove your worth,' I summed up.

'Yes, Shankar, now that you are the CEO of a listed company, you too may need to subtly change your personal brand image. But I can't imagine you at the golf course!' said Kunal, a champion golfer who had won several inter-IIM golf tournaments.

Our coffee had gone cold. We were about to order a fresh round when we spotted an apparition emerging through the mist.

7

What Is Executive Presence?

AS WE ARE ABOUT TO START SIPPING OUR FRESH CUPS of coffee, we spot a jogger approaching the coffee shack. As the mysterious figure emerges from the light mist, we realise it was our batchmate Joe Kurien.

Joe had grown up in a small town outside Kottayam in Kerala and he came to IIM after completing his engineering. After his MBA at IIMC he landed possibly the most coveted consumer marketing job on campus. He served at this MNC for ten years and had a promising career all the way to the top in that job. But after a decade, he was bitten by the media bug. He realised that the world of media was undergoing a great transformation. A large media group hired him to set up their new television division.

Joe and I were good friends both on campus and outside. We were both marketing majors and took many courses together. We used to have our addas at Debu-da's tea shack, discussing memorable ad campaigns and new brand launches. After we graduated, we had jobs in the same city and were flatmates for a while. I knew that he was out for his daily 10–15 km run. An avid runner, he had participated in five international marathons and numerous national ones. He was not terribly tall—maybe 5 feet 8 inches—but all that running had given him a lean and lithe frame. With his chocolatey skin and salt-and-pepper hair, he could well have been in front of the TV cameras.

'Hey Joe!' we yelled in chorus, and fortunately for us, he was not listening to a podcast with his noise-cancelling earphones on, as he usually did. He heard us and slowed down to greet us while catching his breath. We asked him to join us for a cup of coffee and, much to our surprise once again, he agreed. Apparently, he had done three laps around the campus and was ready to hit the sack.

'Good to see you guys. It is all ending tonight! Our silver reunion. Did you guys meet the press reporter I had arranged? Look out for some nice photographs in tomorrow's paper. It has been such a blast being back on campus. We are off tomorrow!' he said as he grabbed a coffee. 'Anyway, what are you guys talking about?'

'Really Joe, it has been so good to catch up with everyone after all these years. Just now we were having a fascinating discussion with Ambi and Rita on personal branding,' said Shankar.

Kunal decided to chip in, 'Joe, you are from the world of media. It will be great to hear your perspective on this stimulating subject.'

'So, you guys were listening to a lecture from our to-be-professor, is it?' was Joe's friendly jibe at me.

'Haha. I am no professor, yaar. And it wasn't just me doing the talking. Actually, Rita knows as much or perhaps more about the topic,' I replied.

'Where have you reached in your personal branding journey?' Joe wanted to know.

Obviously, Joe was a master of product and personal branding. Having worked in marketing for a full decade, he made a smooth transition to the media side. Not only did he launch a very successful news channel, he also added a great deal of marketing brain power to the media organisation, where he was one step removed from the CEO. The family that owned the media group was grooming him to take over the top job once the current CEO retired. So, Joe came with a lot of clout in the world of media and branding. He was also instrumental in creating several successful media properties, or personal branding properties, like the CEO of the Year awards, the supermodel listing, etc. He knew a lot and we were hoping that we could get him to open up and share some of his secrets. At least that was my fond hope. Incidentally, Joe and I had served on several advertising, marketing and media industry bodies together and I always enjoyed the perspective he brought to any discussion.

'We were talking about the importance of personal branding in our new world. How anyone in an organisation can go about building her personal brand. We were trying to convince Shankar that it should not be frowned upon, but should be encouraged,' Rita was quick to add.

'Joe, these two were telling me that I am a brand. And to build a personal brand you have to go through some specific steps. You cannot just say that I want to be a brand and expect it to happen automatically. There is a whole method to go about it. And if you know the method—with various little steps and stages—you will be successful,' Shankar showed off his newly acquired knowledge.

'As you know, Joe, in our finance industry, personal brands are important to get clients and keep clients. But Rita and Ambi were telling us that personal branding is relevant and important in B2B and manufacturing industries as well,' Kunal added.

'Personal branding! What a terrific topic to discuss at 11 p.m. on our last night on campus!' said Joe smilingly. 'Tell me guys, have you discussed the importance of executive presence yet?'

'First ball googly! What is executive presence?' was Shankar's quick retort.

'So, you guys have been discussing personal branding but are yet to talk about executive presence? Is that right?'

'Well, we know what executive presence is ...' Rita trailed off.

I helped her out, 'Really, Joe, we know about it, but did not think of discussing it in the context of personal branding.'

'That's alright. Working in the media, day in and day out we are inundated with media releases, all trying to build personal brands of CEOs. I have realised that the way a journalist reacts to the stimulus depends on their experience with the CEO. And that depends on the executive presence of the CEO', Joe explained.

'But Joe, what exactly is executive presence?' Shankar was now curious.

'There is an old joke about pornography. A judge once ruled that you cannot define pornography. You know it when you see it,' said Joe.

'What? Executive presence is nudity?' Shankar was even more curious.

'Oh boy! Shankar, you have not changed a bit in twenty-five years. I was only making a point that executive presence is difficult to define, to pin down. It's an intangible quality that some people possess, and you can make it out in a second. Is it just the right dress? Is it the firm handshake? Is it the booming voice? All of the above? I don't know for sure, but you will know that a person has executive presence when you see it,' Joe went on to explain.

'It is true that executive presence is an abstract idea, but let me try to explain it, even if incompletely. It is an ability to project self-confidence, the sense that you can take control of a difficult situation. That you can take tough decisions on your own, and that you can be relied upon,' Rita added to Joe's explanation.

'There is a saying that you should not dress for the job you have but for the job you are aspiring to,' I added. 'Executive presence is about the way you carry yourself, your poise and voice, body language, how you communicate.'

'Aah, but sometimes you can go horribly wrong in judging a person by their appearance or the way they carry themselves,' Kunal joined in. 'I once hired this guy from a top business school and he had a great academic record. He was always dressed impeccably and was very well spoken. He was sharp and grasped our projects quickly. But he could not, for the life of him, take a decision without consulting me twenty times. I started getting complaints from my clients. Even his team members were unhappy working with him because of his indecisiveness. Taking a decision meant accepting the risks and the responsibility, and he had zero appetite for it. After some three years of trying to mould him, I had to ask him to look for other opportunities. So, I am sure what you guys are saying is all good, but executive presence is not just about your clothes, voice and body language.'

'Of course, Kunal. You need to have a baseline level of self-confidence, and the willingness and the ability to handle unpredictable situations. That's a given, that goes with the territory of an executive-level job,' Joe corrected the misinterpretation that had emerged in the discussion.

'Look at the new campus hires. Some of them speak too much. And some of them speak too little or hold back. But even at a young age, you can see if a kid has executive presence,' I joined in. 'For example, just last year we hired two young MBAs in our agency. Both quite hardworking and intelligent. But one of them was always unsure about what he was presenting. The other was overly sure. We had to work with both of them to correct them appropriately. One interesting thing we learnt was that getting them to make presentations to clients quickly teaches them how to develop their own executive presence.'

'Isn't that dangerous? Making an unsure novice present to a client?' Shankar was worried.

'Well, Shankar, how will you develop your presence in the absence of an audience? Obviously, I'm not recommending that you send a rookie to present to your most important client. But there are softer targets to give them. We once had a foreign employee working with us on a global transfer programme. That girl had been in advertising for two years and had worked in Chicago and Auckland. But she had never got an opportunity to make a presentation to an external client. I told her to work on a project on her own. I made her present to the internal agency team twice. After we were confident that she could do it, we let her lead the client meeting. The client loved her presentation and it made her day. It gave her confidence a huge boost. I am sure her executive presence went through the charts the next month. She was walking tall for a whole month,' I added.

'One easy target I tell my clients to go after are business schools,' Rita commented.

'Business schools?' Shankar was surprised. 'But IIMC will not allow a young VP to take a session in their PGP class.'

'Oh definitely. Getting invited to a top IIM is a big deal, Shankar. But there are at least a hundred good business schools in India. And they constantly need industry experts to speak to their students. I know of several B-schools where it is mandated that for a full-credit course of eighteen sessions, at least two should be handled by faculty drawn from the industry. And they are not too picky. Even a five-year experience is good enough to wangle an invitation,' I leaned in to support Rita.

'Shankar, the simple rule of thumb with respect to B-school invitations is to never say no. If it is something that fits your schedule, and the institute is worthy of your time, you should accept the invitation. But if not, don't say no. Instead ask them if you could nominate someone from your company to make the presentation. If you make this offer, chances are most B-schools will be more than happy to accept the offer,' Rita added.

'So guys, do you all agree that effective personal branding is incomplete without executive presence? Many things go together to make up executive presence. And there are specific ways to improve your executive presence,' Joe was still pushing his executive presence agenda.

'Joe, how does one improve one's executive presence?' Kunal wanted to know.

'Firstly, you need to have focus. You need to be aware of yourself, mindfully and intentionally. Then you need to understand the concept of body language. How do you stride, do you walk with your back straight and your head held high? I cannot become a six-footer. I have to make the best of who I am. You need to develop the skill to reflect on your habits, start experimenting with various facets of your personality, and see what clicks. I know someone who only wears bright-coloured trousers. It works for him. This other person who purposefully only wore mismatched socks. It even got written about in our newspaper. Practice with support, find people who can give you inputs to improve your executive presence. Learn to connect with people, don't just transact. Learn some simple tricks to impress new customers,' Joe explained.

'Tell me a simple trick, Joe. Something that has worked for you,' Shankar wanted to know.

'Shankar, all of us entertain clients and customers. And we often entertain them in fancy restaurants, perhaps in five-star hotels. What is your modus operandi?' Joe asked.

'Well, I don't have a set practice. I like a few restaurants and I end up going to them with my customers. I also often try out new restaurants that I read good reviews about,' Shankar answered.

'I too like going to new restaurants. But I go to a new restaurant only with family and old friends. If I am trying to impress a client, I always take them to two of my regular restaurants,' Joe replied.

'Why only two?'

'Those are the ones that I know and can be sure of. Imagine, I am walking in with a new customer. Maybe an overseas visitor or a big advertiser. I walk into the restaurant. The maître d' or the restaurant manager knows me, and he approaches us to address me by my name "Hello, Mr Kurien, lovely to see you again. Your table is ready, sir." I make it a point to address the manager by his name and introduce my guest to the manager. But you know what is happening there, right?' Joe smiled as he told the story.

'Your guest is impressed as hell. Mr Joe Kurien is a

big man in town. Even the top restaurant in a five-star hotel knows him and gives him special service. And he is so grounded and warm towards the restaurant manager. Seems like a great guy, I should listen to him carefully. Right?' Shankar was now a dog with a bone. 'That is a terrific idea, Joe. I wish I'd thought of this before my IPO.'

'Shankar, if you were a big advertiser with us, I would have told you all this many years ago. You live and learn, my friend,' Joe was in his element. 'However, having great executive presence doesn't mean you need to speak loudly. Can you think of a movie character who had great executive presence but mumbled right through the movie?' Joe asked.

The movie buff in me jumped at the opportunity. 'Oh come on, Joe, who can forget Marlon Brando in *The Godfather*? I remember the first shot of the film, which is probably five minutes long. And Marlon Brando's first line in the movie, "Why did you go to the police? Why didn't you come to me first?" delivered in a mumble.'

'Bang on! So, to have executive presence you don't need to shout. Marlon Brando's character has great executive presence. But not by screaming and shouting,' Joe smiled as he remembered one of the greatest opening scenes of one of the best movies of all time.

'Wasn't it Theodore Roosevelt who said "Speak softly and carry a big stick"?' Rita added, not missing a beat in the discussion on soft-talking big shots.

'Executive presence is not just about communication. But isn't executive communication important in building one's personal brand?' Shankar wanted to know.

We had all finished our coffee and were on the road once again. We could see the unique dome of the Management Center of Human Values ahead of us. And we decided to pay homage to the centre and the great professor who had taught us about the importance of human values; who helped us understand that management was not just about maximising the profit potential of a company.

8

What Is Executive Voice?

PROFESSOR S.K. CHAKRABORTY HAD TAUGHT MANY generations of IIMC students. He taught 'Managing for Results' and several other courses. His dream project, IIMC's Management Centre for Human Values (MCHV) was conceptualised in 1992 and was finally inaugurated in 1995, after we had graduated. Interestingly, it was set up with funding from corporates who believed in the importance of teaching human values to management graduates. In 1991, Professor Chakraborty had observed, rather prophetically, 'The crisis in business is spiritual.' A feeling that is far widely shared today. Conscious capitalism has become the flavour of the season and some business schools have instituted an oath-taking ceremony a la the Hippocratic Oath taken by those taking admission in medical school.

The five of us went around the circular MCHV building. Our discussion on personal branding was suspended for a while. We remembered Professor Chakraborty silently in our prayers. He was a personal brand par excellence. Someone who had truly found his calling—to bring human values into management education. And the MCHV building stood as a testimony to his courage of conviction.

'Personal branding gets further embellished by executive presence, right, Joe?' It was Kunal starting us back on our path of discovery.

'Yes, executive presence has a cool younger sister too,' said Joe.

'Kya? Younger sister?' Shankar was curious to know more.

'Yes. She is called executive voice!' Joe said with a laugh.

'But you just told us that you can be successful while being soft spoken,' Shankar would not let go.

'Yes, you can be Godfather without raising your voice. But to be a successful executive with a strong personal brand you still need to have a voice and style that is authentic. Your volume may be low, but your voice has to be clear, concise, credible and engaging,' Joe explained.

'So, you cannot mistake decibel levels as leadership voice,' Rita joined in. 'In fact, in HR, we talk of soft and hard skills. Hard skills are things like subject knowledge, technical competence, etc. And soft skills are qualities like attitude, social skills, integrity, communication, courtesy, responsibility, professionalism, flexibility, teamwork and work ethic. And do you know which of these soft skills come out on the top in rating surveys?'

'Must be attitude?' Kunal offered a tentative answer.

'Nope, it is integrity and communication,' Rita concluded.

'There is a saying that hard skills get you an interview call. But you need soft skills to get the job and keep it. Success is based on not just what you know, but how you communicate it,' Joe added.

'So, communication is important. But what about speaking skills? Does that matter when you look at executive voice?' Shankar wanted to explore this topic further.

'Very much so, Shankar. You as a leader need to assess your speaking skills. And before you get up to speak, you need to go through seven steps. Who is the audience? What is the structure of your talk? What is your vocal pace? Do you need to memorise the talk? What interaction will you have with the audience? What is the point of emphasis? And what is the intro and closure?' I decided to chip in.

'This looks like hard work, guys!' Shankar was getting worried.

'Shankar, it is hard work for sure. Which is the reason you need to pick and choose the right forums to speak. But you should encourage your next level of executives and even some articulate youngsters to go out and speak. Nothing better to build personal branding than delivering keynote addresses in conferences,' Joe added.

'The other interesting thing is to have your elevator pitch ready to deliver at a moment's notice. Shankar, tu bata, what is your elevator pitch?' Joe was wanting to make a point with Shankar.

'Gosh, you're putting me on the spot. But if I have a moment's notice, like right now, then I guess I will say, "We are the most trusted makers of automobile gaskets in

India, supplying to the world",' Shankar came up with a succinct elevator pitch for his company.

Kunal suddenly remembered an elevator pitch story that fructified in a million-dollar deal. 'Do you know that a business owner once saw Warren Buffett in the lobby of a hotel? He recognised him because someone else called out to Mr Buffett. Our business owner walked up to him and only said this, "Hi, Mr Buffett, I am a shareholder of Berkshire Hathaway and am a great admirer of yours. I believe that my company matches your criteria for investment." Mr Buffett asked him to send across the details about his company. And would you believe it if I told you that the deal actually went through?'

'Wow, that is a fantastic story, Kunal,' Shankar said effusively.

'There is a bit of a trick to nail the executive voice every time,' Joe started on a new issue.

'And what trick is that?' Shankar asked.

'Well, executive voice needs to be modified depending on the cultural setting. The voice you use in a Japanese boardroom will sound too soft in an American boardroom. The big thing today is that you need to train your executives to be culture sensitive—what is known as culture code-switching,' Joe added.

'Yes, yes. I know that some of our global buyers need to be spoken to differently. Some need to be given expensive gifts. And they, in fact, embarrass us by giving us extravagant gifts. While in most US companies we cannot give anything more than $100 in value. The same applies to our presentation tone and manner,' Shankar commented.

'The other important thing is how you manage your voice when you are with the media. What say, Joe?' I wanted Joe to give us some tips.

'Hey, I can't tell you all the trade secrets. But remember the print or television journalist has one master to serve,' Joe paused for effect.

'Oooh, suspense ...' smiled Rita.

'And that master is her reader or viewer. You need to speak to them with that in mind. You need to prepare well before you meet journalists. They are going to come prepared. Good journalists spend hours researching and preparing for a half-hour interview,' Joe smiled as he said that.

'Really? I would think being the interviewer must be a breeze, since you don't have to talk very much,' mused Kunal.

'Not at all, Kunal. Coming up with insightful, well-informed questions needs a lot of homework. Many CEOs think that young journalists can be swayed by some bravado. And make the mistake of confusing their demeanour with lack of knowledge. I know of CEOs making mistakes by saying things they didn't mean to and then complaining that it was supposed to be off-the-record. Sometimes they get into an argument with the reporter and end up saying things that can get misinterpreted. And giving long-winded answers when a simple answer like "I will get back to you" would suffice. I can go on and on, but I tell all my CEO friends to hire a good PR agency and get them to do media training for every one in their organisation who will be meeting with the media,' Joe added with a smirk.

'Yes, before our IPO our entire executive board went through long media training sessions. But what you said just now Joe was probably more to the point,' Shankar was complimenting Joe.

'Tell me something, Joe. This whole business of executive voice is applicable to leaders who want to build their personal brand, right? What about the younger colleagues? Do they also need to develop their voice?' asked Kunal.

Rita was quick to answer, 'Haan, of course. The new generation, the millennials feel that they know everything and we cannot teach them much. They are a me-me-me generation. It has been found that millennials need to do style-typing and style-flexing.'

'What is style-typing and style-flexing?' Shankar asked.

Rita was prepared with her answer, 'Well, style-typing is the technique to understand your own communication style and how it is being received by others. For instance, you may want to have a strong technical style to all that you do and you monitor how that is being received. Style-flexing is the follow up, to find out how it is working and the need to be flexible to communicate better. If your "very technical" communication style is not working, then are you flexible enough to change it? In fact, training programmes have been created to help millennials focus better on people in particular and not just technology.'

'Millennials are overly focused on their social media. They think that is all there is to build a personal brand,' I added.

Joe stretched his arms behind his back and said, 'Chalo, you guys continue your personal branding walk. If you are just about getting started on social media and the interwebs, then you still have a lot to discuss, I think. I want to do two more laps. See you guys at breakfast.'

Before we could stop him, Joe had taken off and was about to disappear in the thickening mist. I think all this talk about executive presence and executive voice had stirred him to improve his executive stride. I knew that we were on the same flight back home next morning and I had other things to discuss with him.

Shankar had a questioning look about him. And I knew that he had something new for us to address.

9

How to Manage the Digital Footprint?

'WE SPOKE ABOUT EXECUTIVE PRESENCE AND EXECUTIVE voice. But digital technology is changing the way we work. Many companies are offering their employees the flexibility to work from home or, in fact, from anywhere. And this trend grew exponentially during the pandemic. Where does all this presence and voice go in that scenario?' Shankar had a great poser for the three of us.

Kunal decided to chime in with his additional query, 'Well, many financial institutions too are examining how to make work more modular, so that people can have greater work-life flexibility. What Shankar is asking is quite pertinent. I know a company that has been having even board meetings where directors join virtually from several countries. I am also wondering if there is a need to relook at all the executive presence and executive voice gyan we discussed a few minutes ago.'

'Virtual meetings are definitely becoming more and more common, but that does not mean that we need to throw out what we know about building personal brands through executive presence and voice,' Rita said.

I knew that this was a new domain and we all knew very little about how this would shape up in the years to come. There were many contradictory thoughts going through my mind. But I decided to wade in with a question. 'Well, Shankar, what are the key principles of executive presence and executive voice?'

'We just went over that. Make sure you look smart and speak well. And be consistent. Shankar repeated what we had discussed earlier. He, however, followed it up with a question. 'But when doing a virtual meeting, you are reduced to a little box, and sometimes it's just audio. All your executive presence is nothing in a small box, no?' Shankar asked.

'Shankar, even in a small window you can appear like a ghost or a smart executive. I know some managers hold meetings with a brightly lit window right behind them. If they only flipped directions and faced the light, they would look much better and not ghost-like. Or look at the way you dress for a virtual meeting. Some executives are dressed in t-shirts when the rest of the attendees are formally dressed,' I replied.

Rita jumped in with her suggestions on what works in virtual meetings. 'I read somewhere that there are a few key principles of running a good virtual meeting. And those will help you build your executive presence.'

'What are those principles, Rita?' Shankar was now curious. Clearly, he was getting ready to implement some of these best practices for his virtual meetings.

'Some of the principles are simple. When doing a virtual meeting always face the light. Don't have the brightest light in the room behind you. And just because it is a virtual meeting that you are attending from home, you cannot dress inappropriately. Always dress right. Ensure that you find a place in your home that is tidy and will not distract the other attendees. As far as possible, find a room that is quiet or keep putting yourself on mute when you're not talking. Background household noise can't be helped but can be disturbing. Even if you're in your office, you'll be surprised how bothersome white noise can be in virtual meetings. Then there is the nostril problem,' Rita stopped for effect.

'What nostril problem are you talking about? Are you once again making fun of my big nose?' Kunal asked with a half-smile.

'No, not your nose, silly. I have attended meetings where the attendee is showing off his nasal hair. The simple rule is to ensure that the camera of your laptop or your webcam is at eye level,' Rita added.

'Wow, Rita, you are the expert,' I complimented her on the simple hacks she had suggested. 'In addition to these key things, I think you must also ensure that you test the system and the bandwidth so that you don't end up freezing all the time. I always have a backup network to go to and keep doing speed tests to ensure that my internet speed is good.'

'Everything you're saying makes sense. But how can everyone ensure all of the above? Many people live in small apartments. How can they fulfill these conditions?' Shankar wanted to know.

'Shankar, if people are going to attend meetings from home, then they have to find a corner that is well lit and quiet. And investing in a good internet connection and a backup internet dongle aren't big asks,' Rita fired back.

'I think all that we discussed about executive presence and executive voice applies to virtual meetings too. You need to arrive in time and should be able to join the meeting without any technical glitches. You should have done your homework and not be distracted or looking at your mobile phone when the meeting is in progress. Mute your mic when not speaking. Minimise body movements so it does not distract the others. Pay attention and participate. In fact, virtual meetings give us an opportunity to put up our hands or send questions and comments in the chat box. All these can help improve the quality of meetings and our personal effectiveness,' I added.

'I get it now. Some of these are simple things but we may not pay attention to them,' Shankar was nodding in agreement.

'Yes, Shankar. In fact, going forward for a company like yours, that deals with global customers, virtual meetings may be a blessing. And if you run them well, they can improve your effectiveness,' Rita said.

'Absolutely, Rita. I think the virtual world is rapidly changing the way we do business. And those of us who understand these new rules of the game can get ahead of the pack,' Kunal added. Kunal had been doing virtual meeting with global investors.

'One thing that you have to agree on is that these virtual meetings are a damn sight better than those boring teleconferences we used to have earlier,' I added.

'Oh yes! Some of these routine telecalls in my previous job were a waste of time. They used to run for hours and we used to put the call on speakerphone and get on with our work. Only to say "great initiative" or "good point" every fifteen minutes,' Kunal laughed as he said that.

'You know that a lot of what we discussed here may sound basic, but you will be surprised to know how often these simple rules are violated or even forgotten. I often spend time coaching executives on the norms of digital meetings,' Rita explained.

'I think well-run virtual meetings can be a big help. They can save some valuable resources. And from what you guys are saying, the rules we discussed earlier for personal branding and executive presence are applicable to the virtual world too, right?' Shankar seemed to have seen the light.

Shankar's next question was something I had expected much earlier. 'Guys, you have been schooling me about personal branding, but I think we are missing out on one important area—digital and social media. Aren't those essential for personal branding in this day and age? I'm hoping to hear a no, because I hate social media of any kind,' Shankar said.

And we had another topic to unravel.

10

Why Do I Hate Social Media?

WE HAD BEEN TALKING ABOUT PERSONAL BRANDING for over an hour and a half. And it was interesting that it took us this long to get to social media. Given the fact that all of us were of a similar age (over fifty) and came from similar backgrounds, we did not immediately talk about social media when we started discussing personal branding.

I suspect that if I were to speak to millennials between twenty-five and thirty-five, they would have raised the topic of social media in the first five minutes. It is even possible that they equate personal branding with online presence, not realising that personal branding is a lot more than your Facebook profile. This is perhaps why they end up putting the proverbial cart before the horse.

Don't get me wrong. I am not decrying social media. But to equate personal branding to social media posts is indeed, to use another metaphor, missing the forest for the trees. You need to figure out your personal brand before you decide what you want to do on social media. Or if you are already doing random things on social media, you need to pause and figure out what you want your personal brand to stand for and then align your social media activities to your brand message.

I tried to get that across to Shankar, 'In my mind, social media presence comes after you have understood what your personal brand stands for. Not the other way around. You cannot start tinkering on social media and then figure out what your personal brand identity is. The best thing to do is to decide broadly what you want your personal brand to be, try and live that in your professional life and then create a social media presence.'

Rita, who was listening to my little talk on social media, opened a new issue to debate. 'I agree that you need to be clear what kind of a personal brand you are trying to build. And even before you get active on social media, you need to define your digital profile. What is your digital persona?'

'Digital persona? What is that?' Kunal asked.

'Kunal, do you remember I told you about a nasty fight that was brewing between Sunita and Karim in my last job?'

Kunal couldn't seem to recall it, so Rita recounted the whole incident for all of us. 'Well, Sunita and Karim were two colleagues of mine. Sunita was based in Mumbai and Karim was based in Bangalore. They were both very competent HR managers, but they were constantly bickering with each other on email. I used to be marked on the mails and did not want to interfere for a long time. Finally, it became so bad that I called for a three-way meeting and got them to meet each other face-to-face. I knew that both of them were good, well-meaning people. But somehow, they were not being their true selves on email. Things so often get misconstrued when you can't hear the person's voice or tone or see their expressions. I had to tell them to stop the email war and get on the phone to talk to each other every couple of days. I even pulled out an old article on email etiquette and shared it with them,' Rita concluded.

Kunal was nodding vigorously and jumped in, 'I think you shared that email etiquette article with me too. I remember a few points from it. For instance, use email only when it is the most efficient channel you can think of. If not, speak. Secondly, don't send something on email that has errors. I have a rule when I am writing a strongly worded email or a reprimand or a complaint. I don't send the email out for at least twenty-four hours. And before sending it out, I read it again. Another simple rule is to never send an email when you are hungry or exhausted. I have also caught my colleagues not cleaning the trail mail before sending out a mail to an external party. Trail mails can reveal a lot of confidential information. One last issue is that emails stay in the cloud for a long, long time.'

'What about not using ALL CAPS in an email? That should be rule number one when you induct a fresher into a job. They are the WhatsApp generation and are used to shortcuts and abbreviations. They cannot understand why corporate communication needs to be a little more formal,' Rita added.

'Arré, what has email got to do with social media brand building? I am still unclear,' Shankar said.

'Well, Shankar, email, or any form of digital communication, is the first step towards social media communication. If you have bad email habits, or bad digital habits, chances are that they will stay with you on social media too. So, writing emails with ALL CAPS, unless you want to scream at somebody, will creep into your social media posts, creating unintended consequences,' Rita elegantly linked email etiquette to social media personal branding.

'Okay, Ambi, can you give me an example of someone who has done a great job of social media personal brand building?' Kunal asked.

'Oh, there are so many people who have done a great job of it. Anand Mahindra, for instance. He is fairly active on Twitter. He tweets a lot of news about his own company and its products, amongst other things. There used to be a joke going around that if your Mahindra vehicle broke down or you had an issue at a Club Mahindra resort, all you needed to do was tag Anand Mahindra on your Twitter complaint. So, Anand Mahindra's Twitter profile is a lot about business, governance and customer care,' I answered.

'Then there is Harsh Goenka,' Rita chimed in. 'Harsh Goenka's Twitter presence is very different from Anand Mahindra's. He has a youthful presence, making pithy observations with a lot of humour. There is even a book of Harsh Goenka's funniest Tweets.'

'These are the rich and famous. They may have had a big following anyway. What about someone lesser known?' asked Shankar.

'Okay, let me tell you about a good friend of mine and a former colleague at the ad agency. She got interested in social media more than ten years ago. She started a blog, writing about past and present advertising. Her passionately written fortnightly posts would run for almost two thousand words. Quite detailed and rich in information, these posts spoke to all advertising professionals and shared a lot of knowledge. After she'd built a respectable body of work, she started tweeting about advertising. And today she is a very powerful influencer on Twitter. I believe that even the top business leaders follow her,' I replied.

'I don't have too much of a social media presence. I don't even know how to navigate this sphere,' said Shankar, looking lost.

'Shankar, have you done a vanity search?' I asked.

'Yes, of course,' Shankar said, chuckling sarcastically.

I chuckled back and said, 'It's not rocket science, yaar. Quite simply, vanity search is when you search your name on Google. How many results are thrown up? How relevant are they? How recent are the results? If you have somewhat of a unique name, it is easier to have a good search profile. But otherwise, add your company name. So, search for Shankar Shah. If there is a film star or a politician with that name, your profile will be in page 3 or 4. So, modify the search to Shankar Shah Perfect Gaskets. See what that throws up. Let me tell you an interesting story.

'There was a young copywriter who wanted to get hired by a top ad agency. He did not just send his CV to the top agencies, but decided to do something different. He made a list of five of the best creative directors in New York that he wanted to work with. He then bought ad space on their key vanity search words, like John Smith, Kate Altman, etc. So, if he wanted to catch the attention of a creative director called Allison Watson, he bought that word. So, when Allison did a vanity search, lo and behold, the ad from our copywriter would show up at the top as a sponsored link. In that search message our young copywriter just posted a plea saying that he is a talented person looking for a break in the Big Apple. It seems he spent $100 to run the campaign for a fortnight. And he got the job he wanted. How did that happen? Well, folks in advertising and media are constantly searching their own name to see how they are faring. So, Shankar, if I do a search on your name, I should get a profile of your digital presence.'

'That is a really interesting anecdote. I never thought that you could get a job by going after people in their name search results. I should keep that in mind,' added Rita, the HR guru.

'Shankar, you should do a vanity search to find out what shows up. That is one measure of your personal brand. But that need not be the brand you want to project. That is what is out there. For instance, the top ten search results may be pictures and news items of you inaugurating the school in your hometown. That may or may not be what you want to be identified for. So, while you have a presence, you should do a zero-base analysis of what you want your personal brand to stand for,' I added.

'Zero-base planning! Hearing it on campus brings back

memories of our own campus days,' Shankar commented.

'You're right, Shankar, it does.'

'If I have to start today, what should I start with?' Kunal asked a Social Media 101 question.

'You tell me, what should that be?' I asked in return.

Kunal mulled over it for a bit and then said, 'I suppose just as we discussed personal appearance, executive presence and executive communication, social media is no different. So, perhaps I should start with my photograph in my social media profiles. I'm already in control of the photos that go out with our media releases. But sometimes I see a news report or an article with a really old picture of mine.'

'Right, Kunal. Social media starts with your profile in various platforms. And they start with your photograph and your short bio or a write-up about you, what you want to be known for. People even use social media consultants to help them come up with those few all-saying words,' I answered.

'Do you have to be present on social media?' Shankar queried.

'There is no compulsion that you should be active on social media,' I responded. 'But I think you should have an updated profile. It is up to you what you use social media for. You can use it for personal or for professional purposes. Or you can use it to communicate—publicly or privately....'

Kunal interrupted me with his question, 'But how private or public do you need to be?'

'On social media you can decide how private or how

public you want to be,' I continued. 'For instance, you can decide that your Facebook profile is only for close friends and family. You can restrict access to all others. You can choose not to accept friend requests of those who you do not consider close to you. Whatever you share within that closed group stays private. A friend of mine, Vas, is very private on Facebook. I noticed that he wasn't tagged in a photograph that was posted by a common friend of ours called RK. When I asked Vas, he said that he had unfriended RK. Not because they weren't real-life friends, but because he felt that RK shared too many photographs and had thousands of Facebook "friends". This bothered Vas. So while Vas and RK meet often and were very good friends, they are not Facebook friends. Strange, but true.'

'I too have friends who are very particular about who they accept as a friend on Facebook. Plenty of kids don't want their parents to be their Facebook friends. Lots of teenagers have left Facebook since they see it as a "Mummy Daddy" social media gathering,' Rita came up with yet another interesting interpretation of private versus public profiling in social media.

'Absolutely right, Rita. In the case of LinkedIn, you know that it is a platform for professional profiling and you want it to be public. The same with Twitter or YouTube to a large extent. But other social media platforms, like Instagram or Snapchat, can be as public or private as you want them to be. You get that, Kunal?' I asked.

'Somewhat ...' said Kunal. But before he could come back with yet another question, Shankar jumped in.

'Yes, I get that. I feel that a lot of people tend to be on social media just to be present. And they just don't think enough about what is personal or professional, and what is the appropriate platform to share things,' said Shankar.

'Actually, Shankar, there are no hard and fast rules so to speak. It all depends on what you want to do with social media. For instance, I have a friend who is a respected creative director in a large agency who only posts food-related information and pictures on Twitter. Nothing related to his work or family. And he has thousands of followers and he loves it,' Rita replied.

'In fact, digital presence is determined by volume, relevance, purity and diversity. You can be low volume but highly relevant to your target audience. So, there is no one formula to it. Not yet, at least,' I added.

'Tell me guys, what are the dangers of social media? What should we watch out for?' Shankar asked.

'Oh, there is a lot you need to watch out for. But first, be ready to be criticised or even trolled. I remember doing an interview with Rediff.com during the height of the Maggi noodles crisis. I endorsed the brand and said that I have not heard of anyone falling sick after eating Maggi. I had been eating Maggi for many years, after all. A day after the interview was posted online, the journalist called to warn me that the interview is attracting a lot of attention. Of the bad kind. A total of ninety-five comments had been made about the interview. And ninety-four of those were attacking me or the website or the journalist. It said that I did it for money. That I am pitching to Nestlé from my ad agency, etc. None of it was true. Our agency worked for one of Nestlé's biggest competitors. I was not too upset about it and I told the journalist to take it easy. But I am very thick-skinned. Not like the creative director at a Chicago agency,' I answered.

'What happened in Chicago?' Kunal was quick to ask.

'Oh, it seems his agency had fired a few creative folks who had underperformed. They decided to attack their creative director continuously on social media. This went on for a few days, things got nasty, the poor guy could not take it anymore and he quit advertising,' I answered.

'Quit a profession he loved because he was attacked on social media?' Kunal was shocked.

'When I read this story ten or maybe fifteen years ago, I was sure that this level of social media attacks would not happen in India. But I could not have been more wrong. Indians have learnt and mastered the fine art of attacking on social media. The bigger your profile, the more you get trolled,' I filled in.

'So as a business leader, what should be my social media strategy?' Shankar asked.

'Well, Shankar, you don't have to be on social media. So that is the first answer. But your company should be present on social media. It has to monitor, control and, if possible, own the conversation going on about Perfect Gaskets. You need a digital monitoring process,' I started.

'Yes, we have a full-fledged social media monitoring centre in our office. And I believe that global banks and FMCG companies have invested in fairly sophisticated tools to monitor social media conversations,' Kunal came in.

'That's absolutely true, Kunal. Your company has to have a social media presence and I am sure it does have one. As far as you are concerned, you have to answer three questions—is the social media presence for personal or for professional reasons? Is the audience that you want to attract going to be private or public? What resources do you have to manage your social media presence?' I responded to Shankar's original question.

'Shankar, your younger employees must already have active social media presence. Do you have a social media policy in your company?' asked Rita.

'I know my people are active on social media, but what is a social media policy?' Shankar was curious to know.

'Well, there are many risks to allowing your employees to do whatever they want on social media. It is okay to post birthday pictures and holiday snaps. But are they to be allowed to post photos of your new product? Is it okay for them to grumble about their manager on a public platform? Nowadays companies are getting all their employees to sign a social media policy agreement. The employee has to agree not to criticise the company in public forums, reveal product secrets, etc. Of course, they will post messages anonymously on Glassdoor or other such feedback forums. That you cannot control. But you need to monitor them through a robust system. And I have had experiences where some of the best employees reveal something confidential without knowing that they are doing something wrong,' Rita replied.

'The world is changing, Shankar. Today we have youngsters who become celebrities by posting YouTube videos. Some old lady in Tamil Nadu posts cooking videos and she is a YouTube sensation. The guy who posts video under #BeerBiceps is a bestselling author. And there are thousands of such examples. Being a YouTuber or a social media influencer is an acceptable job description today. Stand-up comedians have a fairly engaged Twitter following, and when they get into trouble, they become bigger news,' I added.

'Oh yes, Kunal Kamra,' Rita remembered his fracas with a TV news anchor in an aircraft.

'And many others too. There is a whole breed of what we call micro-influencers in India. There are probably several thousand such micro-influencers, each with a million followers. And these are not cricketers, film stars, politicians or religious leaders,' I explained.

'I love these funny caricature videos by this Bangalore-based girl,' Kunal said.

'There you have it. I think her accent is so genuine sounding that you may think she is a Karnataka native with only a passing knowledge of English,' Rita added.

'Coming back to the topic, what advice should I give to young people in my company on how to use social media?' asked Shankar.

I didn't have a ready answer for him, 'That needs a well-thought-out policy specific to your company and industry. But for starters they have to decide what their personal brand will stand for, and how they can leverage social media to build their brand. They can decide to go professional (and public) on LinkedIn and keep Facebook for personal (private) messages. After that they have to decide how much original content they will create and share, and how much they will re-share interesting things that they come across.

'They also need to keep their profiles up-to-date. I got a message from someone on LinkedIn asking me for some inputs on bank branding. He mentioned that he was working with a leading private sector bank. When I checked his profile, I found that he had mentioned "Looking for a suitable break". I alerted him about this. He replied immediately, apologising that he had not updated his profile in the last nine months,' I added.

'Another important thing that we discussed earlier was how HR teams today review the social media profiles of all their new hires. A global study said that 80 per cent of recruiters check the LinkedIn profiles of prospective candidates. I think B-schools too need to counsel their students on social media management,' Rita gave us the HR view of social media profiling.

'Some companies do a great job of leveraging the social media presence of its employees. Some are very shy about doing it. But when used well, it can be a great asset,' I opined.

'I am still unclear as to how exactly a company should encourage the social media activities of its executives,' Shankar asked.

Rita was quick to take that one. 'Let's try with an example. Let's say you are a paint company. And you create useful videos for your consumers. How to protect your home during the monsoon. Or how to check if you have a wet patch in your home. How to prevent seepage, etc. Now these videos will be posted on the company website, and its official pages on Facebook, LinkedIn and Instagram. And now, you can encourage your employees to share it with their family and friends on their private networks too.'

'But yaar, if it is already on the company Facebook page, millions would have seen it, no? Then will it not be spam?' Shankar asked in all sincerity.

'Well, Shankar, you do know that what your company posts on Facebook is not necessarily seen by all the millions of people who have liked your page. For that you have to pay extra. You may choose to do that. But you may also want the message to be shared by your teams. If the video is interesting, I am sure people will happily share it. You know how some ads get shared on WhatsApp? I often wonder why someone is doing it. Some of the ads are not even that good or even relevant to me. Obviously, there was a nudge somewhere and then it spread,' I gave my view on how to use the network effect.

'True, but please remember that social media is a double-edged sword. Companies need to have a social media policy and this needs to be imposed rigidly. You guys are business leaders, so you should do a vanity search once in a while, or your teams should do it for you. And you should also be ready to untag yourself from posts that are irrelevant and delete inappropriate posts. I even tell some of my candidates that they need to try and bury the bad stuff,' Rita added.

'Bury the bad stuff? On the internet? How do you do that?' Kunal was curious.

'Well, it's not easy. But if you keep increasing your volume, hopefully the old bad stuff will go lower and lower in the search algorithm. As long as it does not show up on the first page, you are okay. At least recruiters will not go beyond the first page,' Rita quipped.

'As far as youngsters are concerned, they are digital natives. They live the Insta life. But even they need to keep prospective recruiters in mind,' I commented.

'Let alone recruiters, Ambi, I know that even prospective clients check out your profile before meeting you. I do that before every important meeting, and try to find something interesting about the person I'm about to meet. I remember before meeting one senior executive who I was trying to impress, I did my search and found that he was a big football fan. Somewhere in our discussion, I brought up football and engaged with this person in a meaningful discussion about the upcoming world cup,' Kunal added.

'Aah, so much can be learnt from social media. I get it. I need to go back and check what is floating around on the internet about me. I wonder what oddities will show up,' Shankar mumbled.

'Shankar, your marketing team may have already done that. And you can start afresh as far as your social media presence is concerned. You may want to keep Facebook purely private, and dedicate LinkedIn as your personal branding calling card. Which photograph or photographs will you use for your profile picture on LinkedIn? How often will you post and what will you post? These are things you need to decide. As a busy executive, you may not have the time to be active on Twitter. So, don't do it if you can't find the time. Maybe you should spend an hour every two days on social media, if you can manage that. You could build a habit of posting fresh content every month, something about entrepreneurship, leadership, innovation, etc. Your team can help you with that quite easily. I know of a friend who has assigned her LinkedIn and Facebook handle to a social media expert. They meet every month to decide what they will post next month. Of course, if there is an urgent message, that is handled pronto, but the social media expert handles all the queries and escalates only the important issues to my friend,' I suggested a way out for Shankar.

While Shankar was processing what I just said, the rest of the group fell silent. The social media discussion had gone on for a while and everyone had a lot to say on the topic. We had all run dry. And did not want to start yet another sub-stream topic.

We were crossing the new teaching blocks and several new buildings that had come up since we had graduated. Just as the world of business had changed dramatically in the last twenty-five years, so had the Joka campus of IIM Calcutta.

After a while Shankar spoke up. 'The various stages of building a personal brand seem interesting. And I feel that encouraging executives to build their own brand through various means may not be bad for the company. I'm beginning to see it now.'

'Shankar, maybe you should get a social media expert to do a webinar for all your executives above a particular executive grade. The simple dos and don'ts,' Rita suggested.

'I think you need to be ready to engage with people when they respond to your posts. Don't forget that social media is a two-way street. You have to respond to every comment. People appreciate that you may not agree with their point of view, or are not in a position to offer a job or help. That is okay. But ignoring a comment or a request is not appreciated. I may be over simplifying this. As Rita has suggested, a specialist may be able to help you and your key executives navigate the social media ocean' I added.

'Yes, that is a good idea,' Shankar nodded wisely. And before he could continue, Kunal had something to say.

'But tell me, Ambi, in our industry we pay a lot of importance to personal networking. Big deals are done by networking. Where do networking skills feature in personal branding?' asked Kunal.

'Oh God! I hate networking. All these "networkers" are just leeches trying to curry favours,' Shankar came on strong.

I realised that we were at a point of inflection.

11

Isn't Networking for Losers?

'SHANKAR, IN OUR LINE OF BUSINESS, NETWORKING CAN make all the difference between closing a deal, getting the right price and being left out of the playground,' said Kunal the M&A expert.

'Exactly! I hate it, because it is nothing but a way for you guys to sniff out insider information and use it to your advantage,' Shankar persisted.

'Shankar, why are you so against networking? Have you had a bad experience?' Rita asked calmly, trying to get Shankar to cool down.

'Well, Rita, when I was a struggling entrepreneur, no one wanted to speak with me. I had to make ten calls to get one answered. Especially from bankers. But now that I am successful, there are so many random people wanting to meet me. Often they meet me at events, those rare ones that I attend. They ambush me, thrust their cards at me, insist that I give them my card. Then badger me with requests for a meeting. As a result of this, I have cut down on attending industry meetings and I never carry my business card,' Shankar replied looking annoyed.

'What if you bump into a potential customer at the industry event? Will you still not give your card?' I politely asked.

'No, if there is an important person who I need to contact later, I ask them for their card. Often they are polite enough to give me their card,' replied Shankar.

Shankar was unable to see the point, so I persisted. 'What if they ask you for your card?'

'Oh, I usually have one card tucked away in my wallet for these situations. My safety valve,' said Shankar.

Shankar's answer made me wonder if he really couldn't see that now he was the kind of person who rarely returned calls. Networking, in his case, seemed to be suffering from an image problem. People who network are of very little value to others. And those who don't network are the ones who can help others. As someone wrote, often networking, with aggressive business-card swiping, is like speed dating. It rarely ends in love. And the general belief is that networking doesn't work well for anybody.

But I kept my thoughts to myself since I wanted to listen to what the defenders of networking were going to say. I did not have to wait long.

Rita was smiling at the interaction and decided to intervene. 'Do you know that networking is a critical skill that we need to teach in our institutes of higher education? I have interacted with junior and mid-level executives from around the world in my previous job, and I have noticed that thanks to their better training and exposure, executives from the more developed parts of the world come across as more confident. They can start a conversation with you in a minute. Our Indian executives are often tongue-tied. They rationalise this behaviour by saying that they are the "strong and silent types",' she said.

'Rita, you were talking about sending your daughter to the US for higher education, right? In many business schools in the US, one critical skill that students need to pick up is the ability to network. I remember speaking at an India-themed conference at a leading B-school in the US. At the end of the conference, the speakers were requested to meet some students over wine and cheese. I was hoping that some of the professors would also be around to do the introductions. But none of them were. The students came up to us, introduced themselves, gave us their cards and started chatting. As we got talking, I asked them if they do this often. And I was told these Industry Mixers were held every Friday. Twenty students were let loose on a handful of guests. I found the concept of Industry Mixers fascinating. Something we need to import into our schools here,' I explained.

'Are you telling me that B-schools are only about networking?' Shankar was getting even more agitated. 'No one taught us how to network and we have done okay!'

'Aah, I think Ambi's point is that if we were taught how to network, we may have done better,' Kunal took that one.

'Shankar, the art of networking can be useful for any one. I know that some habitual networkers can be a pain.

But largely, networking never harmed anybody. And to be a good networker you don't need to learn how to swim or fly. Research has shown that if you are a master at what you do, and exude that enthusiasm, then you will be able to network better. Like we spoke earlier, if you have a good executive presence and good executive voice, you have won half the battle. You will always remember your tailor who spoke so passionately about how he only uses double-fused collars that will never develop a bubble. Or a doctor who took the trouble to explain your skin problem in great detail. It has been found that often people who we may call mavens build good networks. People want to speak with them. And in the process, they give them interesting leads and ideas. There is a fascinating podcast I listened to called *Networking for People Who Hate Networking*,' I added.

'Networking for those who hate networking? Sounds like just the podcast I should listen to,' Shankar said coolly.

'You should. In the podcast, the presenter interviews an Iranian who went on to become a very successful private equity and venture capital investor. Ask me how?'

'Sure, tell me.'

'Apparently, he was a very successful carpet-dealer in the Silicon Valley, selling premium carpets made in Iran. In the early days of the tech boom, some of his regular customers were newly minted start-up millionaires. They loved him for his passion. And introduced him to others like themselves. He invested in some of those companies. He soon discovered he had a knack for it—and the rest is Silicon Valley history,' I smiled.

'I should also start a carpet dealership,' Kunal came in smiling.

'Who you know today will determine who you know tomorrow. Becoming an expert in your domain will incentivise others to have you in their networks. And the more diverse your network, the better it is. The late Professor Bala Balachandran, who set up Great Lakes Institute in Chennai, once said that his network is his net worth,' I added.

'Professor Bala was a true visionary and his heart was in India. Now this might be a really basic question, but what is this network of contacts you are referring to?' Shankar wanted to know.

'Well, who are your network of friends and advisors? In fact, who introduced them to you? And who did you introduce them to?' Rita explained the complexities of unravelling a network of relationships.

'Your network needs to be wide and diverse. Unfortunately, most of our networks are based on old college friends and colleagues. There is a theory that says that most of our networks are based on the self-similarity or proximity principle,' I added.

'Sorry, what? What is the self-similarity and proximity principle?' Kunal wanted to know.

'Kunal, if you were to list the top ten people in your network who you can turn to for help at any time, who would they be? It has been found that most people are comfortable with friends who are from a similar background as them. In your case, they may be our batchmates. Or even people from other IIMs. Or people in your industry. Or people who worked with you in the same office. These are good networks but have their limitations,' I explained.

'Arré, how can you make friends outside your circle? You will know people only like yourself, no?' Shankar asked.

I think he was still not convinced about the power of networks, but the fact that he was asking the question was an indicator that he may be thawing to the concept.

'You will notice that often a very interesting suggestion may come from the least expected place. That person may be a friend from your club, or a neighbour, or an acquaintance at your yoga class. Or she may be in the cultural centre where you are a regular,' Rita said.

'Now that you say it, I remember someone in my gym referring an interesting business opportunity to me,' Shankar commented. 'But I dismissed it as an accident. I did not realise that even this has been studied.'

'There is proven research on the need to have a diverse network of contacts. I will not bore you with that. But do you know how Bill Gates got an entry into IBM?' I asked.

'I know that Microsoft, which was still a start-up then, had been given the contract to create the software to run the early IBM PC machines. I thought Bill Gates must have chased them for the opportunity and got lucky,' said Kunal.

'There is an interesting story behind it. Bill Gates' mother, Mary Gates sat on the board of United Way, a charity organisation. There she got to know John Akers, a senior-level executive in IBM, who was also on that board. Both were giving their time pro-bono and had developed a healthy respect for each other. One day Akers asked Mary Gates about her son. She replied that her son had dropped out of college and was working on something called a "software". Akers was interested in meeting young Bill Gates. And that was the beginning of Microsoft DOS that ran IBM PC. It is quite possible that Bill Gates may have met someone else in IBM and pitched his product. But this story really happened. Interestingly, it worked for both of them. IBM PC was launched in 1981 in record time after the project was green-lighted by the board. IBM unleashed a fabulous ad campaign featuring the Little Tramp, a Charlie Chaplin character. To end the story, John Akers went on to become the CEO of IBM in 1985!' I added.

'Wow, lucky accident it was, wasn't it?' Shankar piped up.

'Maybe it was just serendipity. But perhaps not. People who study networks say that in addition to your usual network, you should try and develop a new passion or a new shared activity. That is a great way to expand your social circle and to meet interesting people who may be mutually useful,' I completed the story.

'Now you know why I play golf every weekend, Rita. That is my shared activity and passion. I meet so many interesting people on the golf course. And I try playing with new people often. It is a bit of a challenge, but hopefully the rewards are commensurate,' said Kunal.

'When using networks, you need to be careful on how to build a series of exchanges. At the most basic level is asking for a favour. At the next level is getting into an exchange process—I do this for you and you do this for me. But it is better to build meaningful and lasting connections; so be a giver and not a taker. Ask about a problem that needs solving,' Rita was giving her husband some tips to use on the golf course.

Kunal looked at her with benevolence and pride, 'You're absolutely right. I should ask what I can do to help, instead of always thinking what I want from a person in my network. Givers have a stronger relationship and reputation than takers. They fare better than matchers or takers, I am sure. I suppose they earn more goodwill and capital.'

'Kunal, there is a concept called reciprocity ring. A group of people meet casually with the condition that each will ask a favour of another. And the other person has to do the favour. In my own case, I don't ask for favours, but I ask for advice. I remember a friend who was moving out of his active job. He decided to meet one person in his network every two days and managed to meet fifty people of great influence over two months. And he did not ask any of them for any help. He just told them where he was and asked for their advice. And as you know, everyone is happy to dispense advice,' I added.

'Seeking advice is a great way to recruit an advocate, Kunal. It makes the seeker look humble, respectful and open-minded, and the giver looks magnanimous in her own eyes,' Rita joined the discussion.

'Which is better? Seeking new contacts or reaching out to old ones?' Shankar wanted to know.

'Well, Shankar, it is never too late to build new contacts, but often we neglect the power of reviving dormant ties,' said Rita, the golf widow, smiling at Kunal. 'I think it is important to note that networking is not just grabbing visiting cards mechanically, and is in fact much more complicated and interesting. I hope we have managed to convince you, Shankar.'

'Well, a few minutes ago I thought that networking was just about buttering up people and collecting visiting cards. I did not know that there is so much more to it. Tell me, how does this play in the context of personal branding that we have been speaking about? How can a young executive build a diverse network?' Shankar asked.

'Networking is part of your personal branding journey. You need to make the right connections and maintain them in a way that feels authentic. Nourish the network by an active give-and-take process. Share and spread new ideas. Tap mentors for support and expertise; this is especially important for youngsters. Learn to pitch in the elevator, on the escalator and during a car ride. Manage your image online and remember to reach out after losing touch,' Rita answered.

'Well, Shankar, as we saw, personal branding starts with you. What is it that sets you apart from your peers? How do you define yourself? And what are you interested in becoming? In that context, you build your personal brand by widening your network. For instance, if I am a bright marketing person in your company, I may want to volunteer at an NGO and help them manage their marketing better.

Finance might be my day job, but my passion for music might keep me active in the music circle in my city. But all this has to be done sincerely. It cannot be a post-it job. You cannot do something that you do not care about. And if you do a shared activity with passion, you are bound to make some new friends and also get your personal brand to shine brighter,' I concluded.

'There is yet another aspect to networking in large companies,' Rita explained. 'I was counselling a young management graduate who had done his summer internship with an FMCG multinational. He was hoping to get a pre-placement offer (PPO) from the same company. But he did not get a PPO. His batchmate, who also interned with the same company, got it instead.'

'Arré, maybe because that person was brighter or a better fit.' Shankar opined.

'Turned out that his project was an intense immersion in a north Indian state to understand a complexity in buyer behaviour. He thoroughly enjoyed the project, came up with some great insights and his in-company mentor thought that he had done a fantastic job. But his batchmate had done a project based in the head office of the company. So, according to him—and I totally agree with him—his batchmate had an extra magic potion working for her,' Rita added.

'What magic potion?' It was my turn to ask.

'Well, the other girl had visibility in the right circles. The HO HR team met this girl a few times over the course of those two months at random office events. And finally, when the chips were down, and they had to make only one offer, they went for the girl they knew,' Rita said.

'So, what is the lesson from this?' Kunal asked this time.

'Kunal, you have worked for a multinational bank, and you know how the game is played. It is important to be visible in the right circles. If this guy had to replay his two months, he would have planned at least two trips to the HO during his internship. That way, the visibility factor might have been neutralised. I know that in an MNC it is important to be visible in the global system. If this means attending some tedious global meetings, you need to do it with made-up enthusiasm. If it means you have to make presentations at global forums, you should do it with a smile. You should actively seek and ask for such opportunities. I have heard stories of how a better candidate did not get the India CEO role just because the HO had not met him enough times,' Rita concluded.

'Rita, they may not be totally wrong in picking the person who had a better internal network. The new thing, as you know well, is what is called the social capital of organisations. And that is built by good networks within the organisation. Companies are spending time and effort to help nurture professional and personal connections among workers to cultivate a spirit of trust. The rewards of these efforts aren't immediate or even tangible. But these investments surely pay off over time. However, with the increasing work-from-home culture, companies are going to have to think outside the usual Friday evening wine and cheese sessions,' I joined in the discussion on internal networks.

To this Rita added, 'I feel the internal networks in companies are often neglected. We used to encourage inter-departmental networking through special teams and break-out activities. I have noticed that a person who is able to build bridges across an organisational silo ends up becoming a more visible, more agile, more respected personal brand. So, I keep telling my own mentees, both young and old, how important it is to build networks within companies. The bigger the company the more difficult it is. But the rewards are also a lot better. Then there are those special connector managers ...'

'What on earth are connector managers, now?' Shankar looked a bit exasperated at all these new concepts and pertinent ideas we were overloading him with.

'Oh ho, Shankar, they are people already in your company. You'll agree that internal networks in companies like yours are important, right? Not everyone is good at networking, but there are probably some who are great at it. They may be working in supply chain, but they may know the development folks very well. They also take an employee-centric approach in identifying the coaching and development needs of their employees. And then they use their broader network to help find their employees the right resources and training. These are connector managers. In fact, they are also better mentors to young managers, and usually have highly productive and motivated teams. All large companies have rigid formal networks. But what is more interesting to study are the informal networks. And the connector managers are often found in the key junctions of these informal networks,' Rita explained.

'It is interesting how you have to build your personal brand and at the same time, use networking principles to embellish and project your brand to the right target audience,' Kunal, the master networker, added.

'Aah, we the agile mobile networkers are back at the MDC,' said Shankar.

12

Are We Back Where We Started?

WE HAD BEEN WALKING FOR ALMOST TWO HOURS ON this misty wintry night, and after meandering around the lush Joka campus with all its lakes and bridges, we were back to where we'd started out from. After our long walk and several cups of tea and coffee, we were quite tired.

We decided to sit on the steps leading up to the MDC building for one last round of discussion. We were all catching morning flights out of Calcutta, and given the long distance that one had to travel from the campus to the Dum Dum airport, we'd probably only get a few hours of sleep.

The salesman in me wanted to find out if I had managed to convert Shankar. So, I asked the final question.

'So, Mr Shah, tell me now. Are you comfortable with this new creed of branding, especially personal branding?'

Rita shot back, 'He better be, or we are taking him for yet another two-hour walk around the campus!'

Shankar laughed at Rita's quip. 'Arré guys, take it easy. When we started, I was a novice but now I am an expert.

How can I not become an expert? With one ad guru, an HR maestro and a finance whiz to guide me. I was just ribbing Ambi when we started our walk,' Shankar admitted. 'I had no idea I was about to be schooled and how. But it was so great to listen to all of you. Thanks to Kunal and Rita, I got a variety of views,' he added.

'Let's not forget Joe, haan! I am no expert in personal branding, so I too learnt a lot from the talk, guys,' said Kunal.

'I'm so happy to hear that. We did dispel plenty of myths tonight, but maybe I should reiterate them once again,' I started.

'Aah, there goes professor sa'ab,' Shankar said, alluding to my guest-lecture stints at the IIMC. 'But please continue, yaar!' he magnanimously added.

'Thank you, sir,' I smiled with a mock salute. 'So, the first myth is that personal branding will conflict with corporate branding. We saw that is not true. In fact, having people with strong personal brands may help strengthen the corporate brand.

'The second myth is that personal branding happens on its own. Again, not true. In modern times, you have to take control of your personal brand narrative.

'The third myth is that personal branding is very different from product branding. In some ways it is, but not entirely. Several concepts can be applied effectively to personal brands as well. Brand mantra, for instance. The first step in branding is writing a positioning statement. In a similar vein, the first step in personal branding is to craft a personal branding statement. And to make what you stand for unique and true.

'The fourth myth is that personal branding gets set in stone and is unchangeable. In reality, you need to monitor your personal brand based on the company and the situation you are in. And make suitable changes. Just as a soap brand can get repositioned over time, your personal brand also needs to be refreshed over time. This is especially relevant if you are changing roles or companies.

'Thanks to Joe, we saw the link between executive presence and personal branding. The fifth myth is that personal branding can exist independent of your executive presence. Not true. You cannot build a powerful personal brand with flawed executive presence. Though they may appear to be very different subjects, personal branding and executive presence need to be seen in the same light. And be it the real world or the virtual world, executive presence matters.'

Shankar, desperate for class participation, said, 'We also met the younger sister of executive presence. Executive voice, right?'

'Well done, Shankar! You do remember your lessons well. Topper type even now,' I smiled and continued.

'The sixth myth is that personal branding is very different from executive communication or executive voice. We saw that to build a powerful personal brand you need to have a powerful executive voice. Not that you need to shout all the time. But you need to have a firm and distinct voice. Both verbally and in writing. Without a distinct voice you cannot build a powerful personal brand. Your unique presence and voice will continue to matter, irrespective of whether your meetings are physical or virtual.

'The seventh myth is that social media is a unidimensional one-way street for personal branding. Keep posting. Keep posting. That is totally wrong. In reality, you need to figure out what you want to do in social media before you start posting online. We saw the difference between personal versus professional posts, private versus public posts.

'The eighth myth is that personal branding needs endless networking. In reality, networking needs to be done with intelligence, not just by sharing visiting cards.'

'Yeah, the shared activity principle,' Shankar added.

I ended by saying, 'Yes, we think that networking is all about going to mixers and dishing out visiting cards. That is really old-school networking. The new way is to discover a passion, and develop a parallel network that may not be in any way related to your business or work. And you'll find that your networks become more interesting and diverse.'

'That was a really great summary, Ambi,' Rita said assuringly.

'Let me conclude by saying that when done well, a personal brand can be a great asset. Yes, personal brands are more abstract, more difficult to build and control. But if we can do this well, then there are immense rewards to reap. And also our companies and businesses benefit in the long run,' Kunal confirmed.

'Okay guys, give me some examples of the all-time greatest personal brands,' Shankar said.

'Bill Gates.'

'Azim Premji.'

'Beyoncé.'

'Sachin Tendulkar.'

'Barack Obama.'

'Rajnikanth.'

'Malala Yousafzai.'

'I think the greatest personal brand ever built was our own Bapuji, Mahatma Gandhi,' I added.

'Mahatma Gandhi, a personal brand?' Shankar was intrigued. 'What makes you say that? I am really curious now.'

'Shankar, you go and catch a few hours of shut eye now. I will send you something I had written on the brand of Mahatma Gandhi. It is titled "Spinning a True Brand". You can read it on the flight tomorrow,' I offered.

'That's a clever title. I look forward to reading it. And thanks once again guys for that wonderful discussion,' Shankar said, standing up and suppressing a yawn.

The rest of us stood up too and yawned in unison.

Rita asked, 'Can you send it to all of us?'

'With great pleasure,' I said, giving her a fist bump. It was time to bring this story to an end. And start the next one.

A Letter

From: Ambi
To: Shankar
CC: Rita, Kunal, Joe

Dear Shankar

I am writing this email to you well past midnight. I thought I should give you a bit of background instead of just sending you the Gandhi article—'Spinning a True Brand'.

I hope you enjoyed our impromptu two-hour walk-the-talk on branding and personal branding. During the course of our walk, we started with a quick round-up of the following concepts:

- What is a brand?
- Can anything be branded?
- What are the advantages/disadvantages of a powerful brand?
- Can people become brands?

A large part of the conversation was hinged around personal branding—the process and its benefits. And it was great to have Kunal, Rita and our own marathon man Joe joining us for the conversation.

In our discussion on personal branding, we looked at:

- How to define a personal brand?
- What is the personal branding journey?
- Should a corporate encourage personal brand building?
- Can personal brands be pivoted?
- What has personal branding got to do with executive presence?

- How is executive presence related to executive voice?
- How to use digital media and social media to build a personal brand?
- How to use networking to build a personal brand?

In the enclosed article on Gandhi's brand, you will see how Mahatma Gandhi built his personal brand (though he probably never referred to the term 'brand' in all his writings) by going through the various steps we explored. He decided to define his core as 'truth'. He then developed a unique presence, one that reflected the common man. He used the power of symbols and music to build his presence. He used communication, in an era where there was very little print media, let alone television or digital media. Finally, he brought it all together by building the biggest network possible, a whole nation.

I do hope that the enclosed article will keep you engrossed on your flight from Kolkata to Mumbai. I hope this 'dream seller' has convinced you about the power of brands and branding. If not, then we can continue our walk on Juhu beach. I'm eager to hear your thoughts on the attached article.

Stay in touch, guys.
Safe travels,
Ambi

13

Spinning a True Brand: Mahatma Gandhi

Lessons in Personal Branding

How do great brands get built? Is it just a series of accidents? Or are there well-laid-out steps to be followed?

Simon Sinek's *Start with Why* is possibly one of the most popular TED talks. It was rated among the top five TED talks ever, and has been viewed more than fifty-six million times. In his talk, on which his eponymous book is based, he speaks about 'How Great Leaders Inspire Action'. The basic premise is that people don't buy what you do, but they buy *why* you do it.

Sinek tells us that a great brand like Apple, created by Steve Jobs, does not tell the customers that they make great computers or phones, or that their computers are easy to use. Instead, they tell us quite loudly why they make computers or phones. And what is the 'why' of Apple? According to Sinek, it may be: in everything we do, we believe in challenging the status quo. We believe in thinking differently. The way we challenge the status quo is by using path-breaking technology, beautiful design, and by keeping it simple to use. We want to make computers simple. Sinek says people are inspired by a sense of purpose or the 'why', and that this should come first when communicating your message to a larger audience, before the 'how' and the 'what'.

Defining Brand Gandhi

If we look at Gandhi the brand, it was built not outside in, but inside out. This is true of computer brands and of personal brands.

Gandhi's central idea was the spirit of selflessness. Throughout his life, he lived and experimented with the philosophy of love, truth, non-violence and non-possession. But he also embodied something else that was even more crucial. And if we were to define it in simple terms, to borrow a phrase from Michel Foucault, it is the courage of truth. This courage of truth is what is reflected in everything he said and did. Full of conviction and void of fear.

What was the personal branding journey that Mahatma Gandhi would have gone through? And what were the tools of communication he used?

Presentation of Brand Gandhi

If you've grown up seeing various photographs of Mahatma Gandhi, then you must have noticed how his attire changed from that of a polished London lawyer to that of a simple Indian farmer.

Did he make the change consciously? And did it happen in stages?

Imagine you have been used to wearing a proper suit all through twenty years of your life. And one fine day you give that up and adopt something that is totally alien.

Mahatma Gandhi made the conscious call to change his dress habits. And he says it so eloquently in his autobiography, 'During the Satyagraha in South Africa, I had altered my style of dress so as to make it more in keeping with that of the indentured labourers, and in England also I had adhered to the same style for indoor use. For landing in Bombay, I had a Kathiawadi suit of clothes consisting of a shirt, a dhoti, a cloak and a white scarf, all made from Indian mill cloth. But as I was to travel third class from Bombay, I regarded the scarf and the cloak as too much of an incumbrance, so I shed them and invested in an eight to ten annas Kashmiri cap. One dressed in that fashion was sure to pass muster as a poor man.'

The power of clothing. Why is it so important?

Semiology or semiotics is the study of how meanings are derived from various modes of communication, including words, images, sounds, smells and, in fact, anything that can signify something to someone about something else, together with their rules of use.

Semiotics as a science evolved in the early part of the twentieth century, but it was only in 1978 that branding and consumer behaviour literature started looking at how different types of information affect our attitudes. Semiotics explained the importance of meaning behind signs and symbols. How they are often seeped in meaning with deep cultural roots.

Mahatma Gandhi understood the power of signs and symbols in the early 1900s. He understood that he had to look and feel like a farmer. Or even an ascetic.

In the Shanmukhananda Auditorium in Mumbai, there is a large photograph of Mahatma Gandhi right next to a photograph of the revered seer of the Kanchi Shankaracharya Mutt, Shri Chandrasekhara Saraswati. One look at these two greats and you can see how they are dressed in almost similar clothes.

While semiotics started finding a mention in books on consumer behaviour and brand-building only in the 1970s, Mahatma Gandhi knew the importance of non-verbal symbols. He realised that these non-verbal symbols trigger emotional responses and guide our actions.

Executive presence starts with how you look and how you dress. And Mahatma Gandhi absolutely nailed this first step. His dressing reflected what he was the embodiment of truth. Of simplicity. Of courage. Someone every poor Indian could identify with. In short, Mahatma Gandhi projected his image of being almost a mendicant, a sage, a poor rural farmer. Someone who was very relatable and approachable, and yet, someone who could be venerated because of his message and his actions.

In his autobiography, Gandhi writes about a dialogue he had with a Hindu religious leader. The religious leader was pained by the fact that Gandhi did not sport a 'shikha' (tuft of hair) on the back of his head and was not wearing the Hindu holy thread. Gandhi explains: 'So long as there are different religions, every one of them may need some outward distinctive symbol. But when the symbol is made into a fetish and an instrument of proving the superiority of one's religion over others, it is fit only to be discarded. The sacred thread does not appear to me today to be a means of uplifting Hinduism. I am therefore indifferent to it.' So, in a sense, he decoded the semiotics of the tuft of hair and the holy thread; how they would send the wrong signal to the poor masses.

The half-naked fakir, as Winston Churchill once described Mahatma Gandhi as, was fully aware of the power of symbols. And dressing down was a conscious decision. As Peter Gonsalves writes in his blog: 'Mohandas Gandhi's personal search for sartorial integrity is a remarkable story without parallel in the political history of the world. To him, clothing was not merely a means to a cultural or political revolution. Clothing was an essential part of his inner quest for truth. From the biographical details ... one can abstract the important insights that shaped the various stages on this solitary journey towards greater authenticity.'[*]

Interestingly, he also started to shun mill cloth to switch to khadi, and in fact created a trend in Ahmedabad for wedding celebrations, where all guests were requested to be dressed in khadi clothes (a new kind of a party dress code).

Experts who have studied dress habits of Indians from

---

[*]Peter Gonsalves, 'Half Naked Fakir: The Story of Gandhi's Personal Search for Sartorial Integrity', https://www.mkgandhi.org/articles/half-naked-fakir.html.

a historical perspective have observed how it is easy to underestimate just how radical Gandhi's appearance and clothing policies were. Not only did he challenge long-established hierarchies through his own clothes, but he also proposed a complete re-clothing of the nation, as well as a full-scale reorganisation of the textile industry. The revival of khadi was central to these aims.

Professor Arvind Rajagopal of New York University has an interesting set of observations on the symbolism of Gandhi's dress or lack thereof: 'There is also the lack of clothing, which is also symbolic—you see his chest, his legs, you see he has the body of a poor man, that is, in fact visible. There is an honesty that is thereby conveyed. Gandhi is using his belly as a signifier, and the vocabulary of the body is insatiable and intelligible to all, whereas the vocabulary of clothing presumes one knows, understands, can afford clothes.'[*]

Mahatma Gandhi also realised the power of other symbols—the charkha was not just a tool for spinning yarn. It was a tool for social and political awakening in the country. He understood the dynamics of a village economy and the drive towards self-sufficiency. He figured out that the charkha was central to that idea, and the charkha became a symbol of self-sufficiency, of independence, of simplicity and of rural India. In 1920, Mahatma Gandhi approved the first national flag with the charkha right at its centre. It was hoisted on the banks of the Sabarmati.

---

[*]Arvind Rajagopal, *Gandhi the Communicator*.

Once again, reinforcing his ability to unearth symbols that have a strong meaning and resonance for the masses.

Let us turn to fasting. He used fasting multiple times in his life for a wide range of reasons, like persuading people to keep peace after communal violence, against untouchability and to draw attention to other moral issues. Fasting is once again a simple form of protest and penance, just as his clothing was the simplest form of clothing worn by Indians. Fasting also has great significance in all religions. So, Gandhi's fasting was also rich in symbolic meanings.

How did he define himself? At the sedition trial which began on 18 March 1922, when asked his profession, Mahatma Gandhi chose not to call himself a baniya, his caste, or his chosen profession, lawyer. He said he was a farmer and a weaver. This once again reinforced his ability to project the right words and symbols.

Mahatma Gandhi had a fondness for Ahmedabad (*Gandhi's Ahmedabad*, 2011): 'I had a predilection for Ahmedabad. Being a Gujarati, I thought I should be able to render the greatest service to the country through the Gujarati language. And then, as Ahmedabad was an ancient centre of handloom weaving, it was likely to be the most favourable field for the revival of the cottage industry of hand-spinning. There was also the hope that the city being the capital of Gujarat, monetary help from its wealthy citizens would be more available there than elsewhere.'*

---

*M.K. Gandhi, 'Founding of the Ashram', *My Experiments with Truth*, https://www.mkgandhi.org/autobio/chap133.htm.

As Narayanbhai Desai, the longest-surviving Gandhian points out: 'While the seeds of Bapu's seminal ideas were sown in South Africa, the roots, the trunk, and the branches all grew in Ahmedabad. Numerous experiments of spinning, weaving, sanitation and education started here'.[*]

It was on the banks of the river Sabarmati that Gandhi set up his ashram. Read that again. Ashram. Not a house or an institute or a farm or a political party. Gandhi's India ashram was originally established at the Kochrab Bungalow of Jivanlal Desai, a barrister and friend of Gandhi's, on 25 May 1915. At that time, the ashram was called the Satyagraha Ashram. But Gandhi wanted to carry out various activities such as farming and animal husbandry, in addition to other pursuits which called for a much larger area of usable land. So, two years later, on 17 June 1917, the ashram was relocated to a thirty-six-acre plot on the banks of the river Sabarmati, and it came to be known as the Sabarmati Ashram. Calling the epicentre of his activities an 'ashram', and also indulging in farming and animal husbandry there, further adds to the nuanced way he wanted to communicate that he was a farmer, not a powerful leader.

Mahatma Gandhi embraced simplicity as his semiotic stance, not just in the way he dressed, or the way he named his place of residence or the various other symbols he created; he also embraced it in the way he wrote.

---

[*]*Gandhi's Ahmedabad: India's Womb* (The Times Group Books, 2011).

Communication and Brand Gandhi

Building a great personal brand is not just about adopting a unique or a modest dress habit. Mahatma Gandhi understood the power of communication. There was no internet, no social media sites, limited mass media. But historians are astounded to see the amount of written material Mahatma Gandhi produced in his lifetime. *The Collected Works of Mahatma Gandhi* runs into more than ninety volumes. Gandhi kept diligently writing in his journals and other publications. In 1903, he founded his own newspaper in South Africa called *Indian Opinion*. After returning to India, he edited a weekly journal called *Young India* for several years, and then another weekly English newspaper called *Harijan* which ran from 1933 until his death in 1948.

Business leaders often need to speak in two or three languages in India. Most of them cannot write a letter in more than one or two languages. It is amazing that Mahatma Gandhi wrote copiously in both English and his mother tongue Gujarati. His autobiography is one of the most widely read books in the world. In both Gujarati and English, Gandhi wrote in very simple language, a literary style in line with the 'why' of the brand Gandhi: simplicity, honesty, transparency.

Modern marketing communication speaks of three types of media through which a brand can communicate with its target audience. The first is paid media—print, television and radio, where you pay the medium to carry your ads. The second is what is called owned media. These are media properties that exist within the domain of a brand. For example, a retail outlet has its own walls as its owned publicity medium. And the third is earned media—media or publicity that is garnered free by the brand, through the power of its own messages. In many ways, Gandhi managed to create his own media—newsletters, journals, books and speeches—and since they were so simple to understand, they got shared, and earned Gandhi extra exposure.

Richard Attenborough, the director of multiple awards-winning movie *Gandhi* released in 1982, says, 'When I began to research in India itself, I discovered that the bibliography on Gandhi is more than any other person except Christ. In addition he was also one of the most photographed people of the twentieth century—perhaps even more so than Franklin D. Roosevelt or Winston Churchill.'*

Today business leaders struggle to write a speech. When asked to write a short article they reach out to their assistants to give them a draft. But Mahatma Gandhi not only was a communicator par excellence, he was also shrewd to create his own media vehicles to carry his message far and wide.

As his editor K. Swaminathan points out, 'Gandhi's literary style is a natural expression of his democratic temper. There is no conscious ornamentation, no obtrusive trick of style calling attention to itself. The style is a blend of the modern manner of an individual sharing his ideas and

---

*Richard Attenborough, Afterword to *Gandhi: A Pictorial Biography*, by Gerald Gold (Newmarket, 2009).

experiences with his readers, and the impersonal manner of the Indian tradition in which the thought is more important than the person expounding it. The sense of equality with the common man is the mark of Gandhi's style and the burden of his teaching. To feel and appreciate this essence of Gandhi, the man, in his writings and speeches, is the best education for true democracy.'

We once again see that, unlike a lot of his contemporaries, Gandhi wrote like a common man and his writings were aimed at the common man. His autobiography is almost too easy to read, just as the man himself was, in some sense. It is his ideas and life philosophy that is mighty persuasive.

Let us look at how he used the power of music to capture the imagination of the nation. Music is a very powerful semiotic symbol in India. All our festivals, weddings and movies are full of music. There are numerous rich musical traditions in India ranging from Hindustani classical to Carnatic to bhajans and ghazals and multiple forms of folk music that varies as you traverse the country. Gandhi understood the power of music and used it to unify a fragmented nation. The songs that were sung in his morning meetings managed to cut across religious boundaries and borders. Several songs that were his favourites, some in his mother tongue, are still sung all over the country. The most favourite of them all was the old Gujarati bhajan *Vaishnava Jan To*, written in the fifteenth century, that he adoped into the roster of prayers routinely sung at the Sabarmati Ashram. Loosely translated, it means, 'Call only that person a Vaishnava or a godlike person, who feels another's pain, who feels another's sorrow, and pride does disdain.' Most children are taught this and other songs that Mahatma Gandhi loved, and many learn the songs without knowing the meaning or even the language the song was written in.

In matters of food, Gandhi had his own idiosyncracies. He was a strict vegetarian and wrote extensively about the advantages and benefits of a vegetarian lifestyle. He had his preference as far as consumption of milk was concerned, preferring goat's milk to cow's milk, maybe again communicating his desire for a simple lifestyle.

Even his spectacles became a symbol of immense power. In the year 2014, K.V. Sridhar, a much-awarded creative director and designer, decided to create a unique font style fashioned after Mahatma Gandhi's spectacle frame. In his blog, K.V. Sridhar, or Pops as I know him, says: 'His glasses have a deep significance to all Indians, when he gave away the glasses in the 1930s to an army colonel he said, "These gave me vision to free India".' Today as we live in a free India we still are slaves to violence, terrorism, untouchability, communalism and many more evils. What better way to celebrate his birthday than to use his spectacle frame to create a unique set of Devanagari fonts. The effort by Pops was written about across national media, but the important point is that even Gandhi's spectacles became a powerful communication medium.

Mahatma Gandhi is said to have observed that, 'Non-violence came to me after strenuous struggle. Brahmacharya, I am still struggling for. But truth always comes naturally to me.'

Let us not forget that Mahatma Gandhi built a powerful personal brand because he always stood for truth in all that he did. He created a hyper-real image that brought the poorest of the poor to him. His messages were simple and everyone could relate to what he was saying. It is probably a conscious choice that he surrounded himself with people who were not like him in the way they dressed, in dietary habits or in other proclivities. This expanded his reach to people who may have viewed him to be a bit too simple.

We, in the world of marketing and advertising, strive to create brands that are true to their actual offering. Mahatma Gandhi offers many valuable lessons.

Gandhi is possibly the most powerful personal brand built in this millennium. Yes, religious leaders have great aura and followership, but as a personal brand Mahatma Gandhi is recognised all over the world, even today. Multiple leaders, including Martin Luther King Jr, Nelson Mandela and Narendra Modi have claimed to have drawn inspiration from Mahatma Gandhi's words and deeds.

To conclude, Mahatma Gandhi employed some of the most sophisticated personal-brand-building tools even before they were studied and defined. I would like to once again admit that Mahatma Gandhi was not trying to build a brand, per se. He was trying to help India attain freedom and, in the process, he created several path-breaking approaches to fight oppression. All this only added to his brand magic and this magic has endured the test of time.

Suggested Reading

Adam Grant, 'Networking for People Who Hate Networking', *TED*, March 2019, https://www.ted.com/talks/worklife_with_adam_grant_networking_for_people_who_hate_networking.

Adele Laurie Blue Adkins, 'Adele on Motherhood, Social Media and Breaking Records', *Time*, 21 December 2015, http://time.com/4155795/adele-time-cover-story-interview-motherhood-25/.

Ambi Parameswaran, *FCB Ulka Brand Building Advertising: Concepts and Cases* (McGraw Hill, 2001).

__________, *For God's Sake: An Adman on the Business of Religion* (Penguin India, 2014).

__________, 'Gandhi, the Great Communicator: Using the Power of Semiotics', in Srinivasan Swami and Ramesh Narayan (eds), *Mahatma Gandhi: The Great Communicator* (IAA—India Chapter Publications, 2016).

David Aaker, *Building Strong Brands* (Free Press, 1996).

David Glen Mick, 'Consumer Behaviour and Semiotics: Exploring the Morphology of Signs, Symbols, Significance', *Journal of Consumer Research*, 1986.

David Lidsky, 'These 10 Personal Branding Giants Created Our Influencer-happy World', *Fast Company*, 14 June 2018, https://www.fastcompany.com/40572089/10-pioneers-of-personal-branding.

Emma Tarlo, *Clothing Matters: Dress and Identity in India* (The University of Chicago Press, 1996).

Irving Rein, Philip Kotler, Michael Hamlin and Martin Stoller, *High Visibility: Transforming Your Personal and Professional Brand* (McGraw Hill Education, 2006).

James B. Twitchell, 'The Ungrateful Dead', *Advertising Age's Creativity*, 2000.

Jean-Noel Kapferer, *Strategic Brand Management* (Kogan Press, 1992).

Joseph S. Alter, 'Gandhi's Body, Gandhi's Truth: Nonviolence and the Biomoral Imperative of Public Health', *The Journal of Asian Studies*, 1996.

Kevin Lane Keller, Vanita Swaminathan, Ambi Parameswaran and Isaac Jacob, *Strategic Brand Management: Measuring Building and Managing Brand Equity* (Pearson Education, 2020).

Mohandas Karamchand Gandhi, *An Autobiography or the Story of My Experiments with Truth* (Navjivan Publishing House, 1925).

Naomi Klein, *No Logo* (Fourth Estate, 1999).

Oliver Burkeman, 'What's Good for the Stars is Good for Gandhi', *The Guardian*, 9 February 2002, https://www.theguardian.com/world/2002/feb/09/oliverburkeman.

PAR Marketing Services, 'Branding', White Paper, http:// parmarketingservices.com/Docs/Branding%20White%20 Paper.pdf.

Paul John and Robin David, *Gandhi's Ahmedabad: The City that Shaped India's Soul* (Times Group Books, 2011).

Peter Gonsalves, 'Half Naked Fakir: The Story of Gandhi's Personal Search for Sartorial Intergrity', *Gandhi Marg*, 2019, https://www.academia.edu/2262696/_HALF-NAKED_FAKIR_The_story_of_Gandhi_s_personal_search_for_sartorial_integrity.

Ramachandra Guha, *Makers of Modern India* (Penguin India, 2010).

————, *Gandhi Before India* (Penguin India, 2013).

————, *Gandhi: The Years that Changed the World, 1914–1948* (Penguin India, 2018).

Richard Attenborough, 'Afterword', in *Gandhi: A Pictorial Biography*, text by Gerald Gold (Newmarket Press, 1983).

Rita Clifton and John Simmons, *The Economist: Brands and Branding* (Economist Books, 2003).

Ron Ashkenas, 'Define Your Personal Brand with Simple Questions', *Harvard Business Review*, 22 January 2010, https://hbr.org/2010/01/define-your-personal-brand-wit.

Salman Rushdie, 'Mohandas Gandhi', *Time 100—Leaders & Revolutionaries* (Time Inc., 1998).

Shrikrishna Kulkarni, 'Gandhiji: My Great Grandfather— An Effective Communicator', in Srinivasan Swami and

Ramesh Narayan (eds), *Mahatma Gandhi: The Great Communicator* (IAA—India Chapter Publications, 2016).

Simon Sinek, *Start with Why: How Great Leaders Inspire Everyone to Take Action* (Porfolio Books, 2011).

Srikant Datar, 'Design Thinking Talk', *SPJIMR–SBAC Seminar*, Mumbai, 2019.

'The Case for Brands', *The Economist*, 8 September 2001, https://www.economist.com/leaders/2001/09/06/the-case-for-brands.

Tom Peters, 'The Brand Called You', *Fast Company* (31 August 1997).

William Mazzarella, 'Branding the Mahatma: The Untimely Provocation of Gandhian Publicity', *Cultural Anthropology*, vol. 25, no. 1 (February 2010), pp. 1–39.

Acknowledgements

WHEN THE GOVERNMENT OF INDIA ANNOUNCED A lockdown on 25 March 2020, one of the first calls I got was from IIT Madras Alumni Association (IITMAA). They wanted me to do an online session on branding. I suggested that IITMAA should do these online sessions more frequently (during the lockdown) and that got me into further trouble. They wanted me to do three sessions on branding over three evenings. I did one on 'Branding 101' and followed that with one on 'Living the Brand' (for organisations) and 'Personal Brand Building'. The sessions went well and we had a large number of participants on all three days. Interestingly, those pro-bono sessions got me several more paid (and unpaid) engagements and many of them were for a session on personal branding.

This got me thinking. I have written ten books on various subjects, including brand management, advertising, consumer research and religiosity-consumer behaviour. Is there a need for a book on personal branding, with a strong Indian flavour? My search led me to numerous books written by Indian and international authors. All of them were very useful but I wondered, what if I approached the topic from a different angle. What if it was a conversation?

I had a preliminary chat about the idea of a conversational book with my friend and literary agent Anish Chandy: a book about personal branding which is a heated argument among friends, with its own believers and non-believers. To give it context, I decided to set the discussion at the Indian Institute of Management Calcutta (IIMC) campus. And during the first six months of the lockdown and work-from-home confinement, I wrote the first draft. I had graduated from IIMC in 1979 and had served as a member of the Board of Governors of IIMC from 2007 to 2017. I, however, wanted to set the conversation not in the 1970s but in the 1990s; hence during the course of writing the book I also spoke with a few IIMC alumni, including Sankaran Naren, to ensure that I was not getting any of the IIMC campus details wrong. Thanks to all of them for their inputs. My wife Nithya, who is always quite forthright with her views, thought the book made interesting reading.

Anish Chandy got to look at the first draft and felt that the book would work. The next person to read the book was Karthik Venkatesh who was then an editor at the erstwhile Amazon Westland company. The book got a green light and I was on my way to reworking on my first draft.

As the book took shape, I wanted to pay my own little homage to the father of the nation, Mahatma Gandhi, as the country was approaching its seventy-fifth year of Independence. A chapter was added at the end to give the readers a new prism to look at Mahatma Gandhi.

The book was seen to be a relatively light read; hence the idea of including illustrations to open up each chapter. Thanks to Saurabh Garge for the illustrations.

The search for the title got me exchanging ideas with Anish and Karthik. We honed in on the title. Special thanks to Gavin Morris for the terrific cover design.

When the Westland Pratilipi venture was announced, I was delighted to be approached by Karthika V.K. and Gautam Padmanabhan for the rights to publish this book. They have been great supporters of my previous two books and I am grateful for their support.

Special thanks to Sonia Madan for a thorough edit of this final version.

The Westland team and the PR agency, Moe's Art, have been a great source of support and help. My previous two books, *Sponge: Leadership Lessons I Learnt from My Clients* and *Spring: Bouncing Back from Rejection* have both been well distributed and supported in media with book reviews, book extracts, online reviews, book talks and podcasts. With all that encouragement and support *Spring* made it to the shortlist of the Tata Literature Live! Business Book of the Year Award, 2021. I look forward to all their continued support to make this book a success.

Most importantly, book buyers and friends/colleagues/ students who attend my talks, follow me on social media and provide valuable inputs need my special thanks.

I admit this book is very different from all my previous books (oops, that is a cliché!). But weaving personal branding concepts into a light-hearted conversation among friends is not something I would have attempted twenty years ago when my first book of brand building advertising cases was published. I enjoyed researching the topic (personal branding) and writing this book. I do hope you enjoy the book and will become motivated enough to start having a conversation around personal branding with your friends.

FCB Ulka Brand Building Advertising: Concepts and Cases

Understanding Consumers: Building Powerful Brands Using Consumer Research

Building Brand Value: Five Steps to Building Powerful Brands

Ride the Change: A Perspective on the Changing Indian Consumer, Market and Marketing

DraftFCB + Ulka Brand Building Advertising: Case Book II
(with Kinjal Medh)

Strategic Brand Management
(with Kevin Lane Keller, Vanitha Swaminathan and Isaac Jacob)

For God's Sake: An Adman on the Business of Religion

Nawabs, Nudes, Noodles: India Through 50 Years of Advertising

Sponge: Leadership Lessons I Learnt from My Clients

Spring: Bouncing Back from Rejection